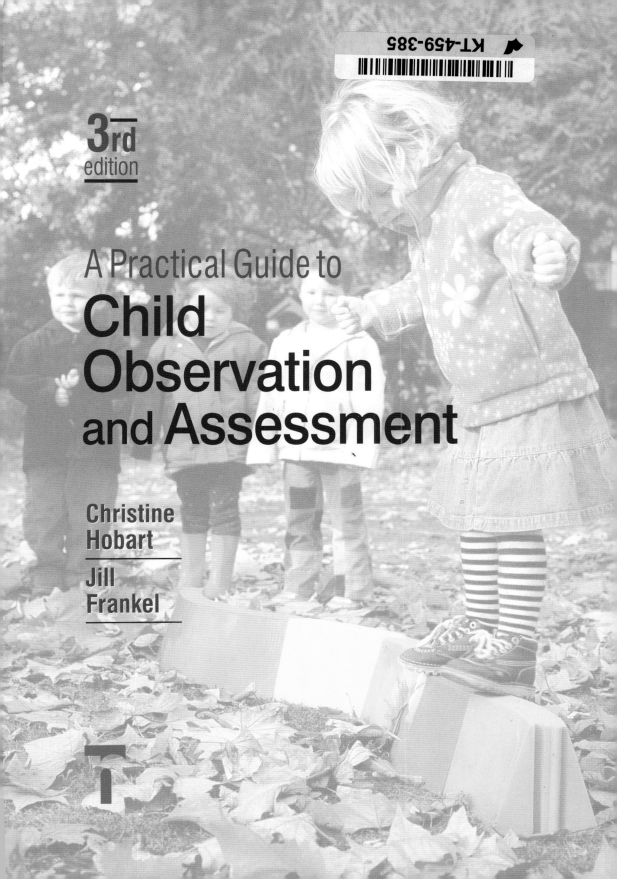

3rd edition

A Practical Guide to
Child
Observation
and Assessment

Christine
Hobart

Jill
Frankel

First edition published 1994 by Stanley Thornes (Publishers) Ltd
Second edition published 1999 by Stanley Thornes (Publishers) Ltd

This edition published 2004 by:
Nelson Thornes Ltd
27 Bath Road
Cheltenham GL53 7TH
United Kingdom

04 05 06 07 08 / 10 9 8 7 6 5 4 3 2 1

A catalogue record for this book is available from the British Library.

ISBN 0 7487 8526 4

Cover photograph: Martin Sookias
Typeset by Florence Production Ltd, Stoodleigh, Devon
Printed and bound in China by Midas Printing International Ltd

Contents

About the authors

The authors come from a background of nursery teaching and health visiting, and have worked together for many years training students to work with young children. They have written twelve books encompassing all areas of the childcare curriculum.

Acknowledgements

The authors would like to thank colleagues and students in the Child and Social Care Programme Area at City and Islington College for their support and encouragement.

We would also like to thank Mine Conkbayir, a student from City and Islington College, and Elizabeth Hart, Elizabeth Gormley and Sarah Clarke from Oaklands College for allowing us to use some of their observations in the book.

Many thanks to the staff and children at Treetops Nursery, Cheltenham for their time and enthusiasm during the photoshoot.

The authors and publishers are grateful to the following for granting permission to reproduce copyright material:
- ERIC Clearinghouse on Elementary and Early Childhood Education (pages 106–107).
- Margaret O'Donovan (the baby study outline, page 148).
- Hannah Mortimer (pages 74–76).
- D.E. McClellan and L.G. Katz (page 77).
- Sheffield LEA (1992), *Nursery Education: Guidelines for Curriculum, Organisation, Assessment*, Sheffield. Available from Early Childhood Education Centre, Strand House School, Queen Mary Road, Sheffield S2 1HX (pages 78–80).
- Alison Mitchell ('Activity', page 139).
- High/Scope UK, 192 Maple Road, London SE1 8HT (pages 140–143).
- Child Growth Foundation (percentile chart, page 150). Copies of percentile charts may be purchased from Harlow Printing, Maxwell Street, South Shields NE33 4PU.
- Professor Sheila Wolfenden, *All About Me*, published by NES Arnold, 2nd edition, 1998 (page 72).
- Theo, Victoria and Hampden Square Nursery School, for the Post-it notes (pages 152–153).
- The QCA for the abstract from the Foundation Stage Profile (page 151).

Every effort has been made to contact copyright holders, and we apologise if any have been overlooked. Should copyright have unwittingly been infringed in this book, the owners should contact the publishers who will make corrections at reprint.

1 An introduction to child observation

This chapter covers:

- The professional role and responsibilities of the childcare and education practitioner
- The student as scientist
- Perception: the act of interpreting our senses
- Objectivity and bias
- Cultural bias
- Feelings and anxieties

Learning outcomes

Students on many childcare and education courses are asked to observe children in a meaningful way on a regular basis, building up a portfolio of observations and assessments which will lead to an understanding of the development and needs of children. This should be carried out with sensitivity, objectivity and an awareness of anti-discriminatory practice.

Observing children is different from being alert and noticing what is happening around you. Professional observations have a focus and are carried out in order to plan for and assess children in a purposeful manner. This allows students to understand fully their own professional role as childcare and education practitioners, and gain a true insight into good practice in the workplace.

The professional role and responsibilities of the childcare and education practitioner

At your centre you will be learning the theory of normal child development and growth and understanding children's needs. By the practice of closely observing children, you will integrate this theory with what you are observing in the establishment. Further discussion in your group with other students, and your tutors, will allow you to see how they have observed similar situations. You will become aware of the great variety and range in the development and needs of children.

Throughout your training the concept of professional behaviour will be emphasised both in the workplace and at your centre. This touches every area of the work you do.

During the period of your training, as well as acquiring a body of knowledge you will reach an understanding of accepted professional behaviour and attitudes. If you are an NVQ candidate you will also be recording your observations of children, storing them in your portfolio for discussion with your assessor.

Observations play a part in helping you to gain knowledge and understanding, and you will learn to interpret your observations in such a way as to assess children's development and meet their needs. With regard to observations, you must be aware of your responsibility to recognise the rights of parents, colleagues and children.

The 1989 United Nations Convention on the rights of the child sets out 54 Articles. The Articles that relate particularly to observing children are:

- Article 12: Children have the right to say what they think should happen when adults are making decisions that affect them, and to have their opinions taken into account.
- Article 13: Children have the right to receive and to share information, as long as the information is not damaging to them or to others.
- Article 16: Children have a right to privacy. The law should protect them from attacks against their way of life, their good name, their families and their homes.

It should be made clear to the parents by the school or the nursery that observations will be made of all the children from time to time, so that the staff can assess and evaluate the children's progress. These observations will be made by the staff team and occasionally by students placed in the establishment for their practical training.

Activities

1   It has been suggested that children from five years upwards should give their consent to students who wish to observe them. How might this affect the observation?

2   By undertaking observations of children how might you
    - protect them?
    - aid their development?
    - encourage their participation in play and learning?

3   Discuss within your group if you think there is a conflict of interest in observing children, recording these observations, and their right to privacy.

You will share your observations with members of the childcare and education team, so as to enrich their knowledge of the children, whilst gaining insight from them into the children's development and behaviour. You may have the opportunity to share your observations and record keeping with a child's parent. Involving parents in this process may result in a contribution from their primary knowledge of their own child, and this will result in a more reflective and sensitive assessment of the child.

Sharing observations with a parent

Data Protection Act

All establishments holding personal data stored electronically on computers or on CCTV tapes must comply with the provisions of the Data Protection Act 1988. This would include health details, family information and observations and assessments of the children.

There are eight data protection principles, which require that all information is

- fairly and lawfully processed
- processed for limited purposes
- adequate, relevant and not excessive
- accurate
- not kept longer than necessary

- processed in accordance with the individual's rights
- secure
- not transferred to countries outside the European Community without adequate protection.

Individuals are now empowered by law to access information that is held about themselves on computer and some paper records such as school and medical records. Any establishment receiving a request would be obliged to respond positively and promptly. The individual can apply to the court to alter or destroy personal details if they are inaccurate or biased. All students should discuss with their supervisor or assessor how the establishment implements data protection and what is required of them when recording observations and writing assessments.

You will become aware of much confidential information concerning the children and their families. The amount of information disclosed to you will depend on what is necessary to meet the needs of the child, and to help you to function within the team and gain a deeper understanding into working with families. All information that you receive, either written or verbal, is strictly confidential. You should never share it with your family and friends. Even your tutors will not want you to reveal the identities of the children that you observe in your placement. Your observations should show awareness of and empathy with the needs of children and their families regardless of race, class, culture, religion, disability, gender, sexual orientation or age, both individually and in groups. You should show respect and interest in the customs, values and beliefs of all the children whom you observe.

The student as scientist

All scientists collect data to test hypotheses from which to construct or test theories. For example, a scientist wanting to find out why there are fewer butterflies in a certain area of England might well present a hypothesis that the reason is a change in the climate, as there is not as much vegetation around for the butterflies to feed on. She will then need to observe the habitat closely, regularly monitor the number of butterflies and compare the food supply with that of another area in which there are more butterflies. Having collected all these data, the scientist may be able to show that the data either support or disprove the hypothesis.

In the same way, using a scientific method, you will collect data on child development and behaviour which will allow you either to confirm preconceived ideas you might have had about children or to alter your thinking in some areas. This approach demands objectivity – remaining detached from what you are observing and not allowing yourself to become involved as this may lead you to influence the outcome. This is not always easy as we are inclined to make emotional responses to children, but as time goes on you will learn to stand back and be objective in your observations.

Perception: the act of interpreting our senses

Perception is more than just seeing. It is our individual interpretation of what we see, hear, taste, smell and touch.

How many legs does the elephant have?

Are the rows parallel?

A Practical Guide to Child Observation and Assessment

Look at the chart and say the <u>COLOUR</u> not the word

YELLOW BLUE ORANGE
BLACK RED GREEN
PURPLE YELLOW RED
ORANGE GREEN BLACK
BLUE RED PURPLE
GREEN BLUE ORANGE

Left – Right Conflict
**Your right brain tries to say the colour but
your left brain insists on reading the word.**

Look at the drawings above. What do you see? Perhaps some of the students in your group will see a different picture from the one you see. It is not always easy to rely on our eyes. How do we know that what we see exists? Do we introduce things from our imagination? For example, after a hold-up in a bank, the police will question the eyewitnesses as to what happened and what the criminals looked like. In general, no two descriptions are ever completely the same. People's perceptions are coloured by their past experiences, expectations, desire to please, possible fears and anxieties, and even last night's television viewing.

Trying to observe children objectively, so that you are able to convey your data clearly to other people in a way that they can understand, sometimes seems an almost insurmountable task. As in every other area of observation skills, you will progress in time and with practice. Often what is important to you can dominate the observation. You must take care not to generalise from your own individual experiences and expectations when observing children. Your interpretation of any observation needs to be based on the knowledge and understanding that you are gaining in your academic work and in your work with children.

Activities

1   Sit down with two or three other people to watch a particular current affairs programme. Write down what you see as the six most important points made during the programme. Compare your lists. Did you all agree on the most important points? Did your lists vary? Why do you think this was?

2   If you are part of a class group, ask two students to role play a childcare and education practitioner reading to a child. The rest of the group will record what is happening. Read out your observations. Did all the members of the group have similar recordings?

Objectivity and bias

You need to be careful when you observe children that you are entirely objective and unbiased. This means that you write your observations in a detached and impartial manner being sure that you are not influenced by prior knowledge of the child or the family, your personal feelings towards the child and your expectation of her behaviour and development.

Many factors might affect your observations. Preconceived ideas about the character or competence of individual children may influence your record keeping. Expecting a child to succeed in a task may prevent you recording accurately a lack of attainment. Knowing a child to come from an apparently happy and stable home might lead you to reject an observation showing a child at risk.

The familiarity or otherwise of the setting should be borne in mind. A child observed playing while waiting for a dental appointment would possibly not be as relaxed as a child playing in the familiar surroundings of the placement or the home.

Environmental factors, such as sudden hot and sticky weather or rain for days at a time, may well cause behaviour which is unusual, and should be noted in any observation. Difference in noise levels is unsettling for everyone, children and observer alike. Changes in routines, such as outings or visitors or staff changes, must also be recorded.

You must be sure that your observations are always a true record of what is taking place and that you are not tempted to add anything which might make them more interesting and easier to interpret. If you are assessing children's physical skills, such as the ability to skip, you must ensure that you ask them in a neutral fashion to demonstrate the skill and that you ask all the children in the same way.

A Practical Guide to Child Observation and Assessment

If you are having difficulty in always being objective and being sure that you do not demonstrate any bias, discuss this with your supervisor or assessor. Some supervisors might find the time to observe a child at the same time as you, comparing records afterwards. This may help you to look at children and situations with more objectivity in the future.

You may find yourself working in the same placement room as another student, and this might help you to check the reliability of your observations by both of you observing the same child at the same time and using the same technique. If 85 to 90 per cent of your recording agrees, it can be seen to be reliable.

Cultural bias

You also need to be aware that many of the children you observe may have been brought up in a different culture from your own, which may have different expectations of children's behaviour. For example, a child who never says 'Thank you' when offered help might not have the words for this in their home language. Some children may dislike messy play because this has been positively discouraged at home; others may be very articulate as they have spent a great deal of time with adults. Yet again, some children from another culture will not look an adult in the eye as this is seen as disrespectful.

 ### Activity

In groups of four, identify five different cultures and compare possible differences in family size, moral codes, diet, eating patterns and dress. Speculate how some of this knowledge might have an impact on your observations and interpretations.

The greater the understanding and knowledge that you have of other cultures the less likely you are to make value judgements based on your own upbringing and background. The practice of reading and discussing your observations in class will help you to become more aware. What we choose to observe may be a matter of personal bias. Some people might be more interested in language development and record many examples of conversations with children, whilst others might concentrate on social development, recording friendships and social skills. To complete a satisfactory portfolio, a whole range of observations needs to be recorded.

An observation is simply a sample of behaviour or development and you must be careful not to use it to plan for the child until you have confirmed your findings by doing several more observations. One observation will never give you a total picture.

Storytime

Activity

Tutors at an observation training day identified the skills needed by childcare practitioners in order to observe children successfully.

Complete the table on page 11, assessing yourself at the start, midway and at the end of your course.

Looking at this list, what skills do you think are essential at the beginning of the course, and which ones might you develop during the course?

Feelings and anxieties

It is quite natural to feel anxious and apprehensive at the start of a new course and, in particular, at the thought of being asked to do observations. Past students may have taken pleasure in telling you how complicated they are. With the help of your tutor and placement supervisor, you will soon make progress and even enjoy using various techniques. Observing children in the placement will help you understand

Observation skills

	Start	Midway	End
Ability to evalute			
Ability to negotiate time to observe			
Ability to note detail			
Ability to plan			
Ability to take notes and record information			
Communication skills			
Confidence to make a start			
Good interpersonal skills			
Knowledge of child development			
Knowledge of observation techniques			
Listening skills			
Maturity			
Objectivity			
Patience			
Sensitivity			
Time management skills			
Understanding of aims			
Unobtrusiveness			

the theory of child development and care, and is the best way of integrating theory with practical work.

You may have been brought up not to stare at people, and certainly not to write down things about them in their presence or to make comments about their behaviour. Some students will feel that observing children is intrusive and feel awkward recording what they see. However, you will be working within strict professional codes of behaviour and within the bounds of confidentiality. If you have these worries, talk frankly about them to your tutor. You will be reassured that these observations are often put to very good use, allowing supervisors to promote the development of the children in their care and to ensure that all their needs are met.

It is possible that you may see an example of bad practice and wonder whether to record this or not. In all cases the observations should be about the child, or group, that you are watching, and bad practice recorded only if the child or children react to it. For example, you might record that a group of children were sitting at the dinner table for 15 minutes before the meal arrived, having taken an equally long time to wash their hands and get ready. You might feel that a lot of time had been wasted, but it is the children's reaction to the situation that is important. Most supervisors, being professionals, will react well to constructive criticism, but if you have any real concerns you will obviously discuss the matter first with your tutor or assessor.

You may find it very worrying if you record something about a child which might reflect on the parents or the child's family; for example, a child who is very upset because they have not been collected from the nursery on time. Parents have a right to see any observations about their children, and you must always keep this in mind. Your supervisor will give you guidance on this.

Very occasionally, through language samples or observation of behaviour, students identify children who may be being abused in some way. This concern must be shared immediately with your supervisor or line manager, who will take the appropriate action. You should also discuss this with your tutor, who will endeavour to support you.

2 Why we observe children

This chapter covers:

- Normal child development and growth
- Understanding children's needs
- Social interaction with children and adults
- Changes in behaviour
- Healthcare and safety
- Record keeping and future planning

Learning outcomes

In your centre your tutors will be teaching theories of child development, education, health and childcare within a framework of social studies. Instead of learning this in a vacuum, you are fortunate in spending a great deal of time observing children and practising your skills using your ever-increasing knowledge.

The exercise of observing and assessing children formalises the link between theory and practice, so that you are able to demonstrate what you have learned about children in all areas. For example, your understanding of a child's readiness to reach out and grasp an object at about four months will be confirmed when observing a child of this age reaching out for a toy. Observing a two-year-old starting to put sentences together will help you understand the sequence of language development.

'I hear: I forget. I see: I remember. I do: I understand'

(Chinese saying)

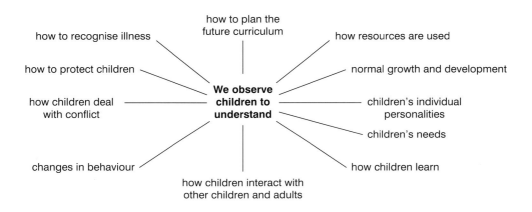

how to plan the future curriculum

how to recognise illness

how resources are used

how to protect children

normal growth and development

how children deal with conflict

We observe children to understand

children's individual personalities

children's needs

changes in behaviour

how children learn

how children interact with other children and adults

Normal child development and growth

Many of your observations will be about normal child development and you will need to understand how children develop in several areas.

Physical development: this is divided into *gross motor development* – how children grow and acquire physical skills, from gaining head control to full agility; for example, look for a child or children

- riding wheeled toys
- climbing
- trampolining
- digging
- throwing balls
- swimming

– and *fine motor development* linked with vision and hand–eye coordination; for example, look for a child or children

- threading beads
- drawing
- tying a shoelace
- sewing
- using a computer keyboard
- doing a jigsaw

Intellectual/cognitive development: the development of children's ability to think and learn through interacting with their senses and experiences; for example, look for a child or children

- reading
- telling jokes
- explaining a recipe
- making models
- reciting rhymes
- concentrating on a project

Language development: from the first cry, through the growth of verbal communication skills, to true speech and understanding; for example, look for a child or children

- holding a conversation with an adult
- listening and responding to a tape
- holding a conversation with another child
- being assertive
- following instructions
- explaining a project

Emotional development: from initial total dependence to full independence and autonomy; for example, look for a child or children

- having a tantrum
- being competitive
- being shy or withdrawn
- separating from parents on arrival
- showing affection
- showing aggression

Social development: from close bonding to full and rich relationships with a complex network of children and adults; for example, look for a child or children

- caring for another child
- taking part in a group story
- planning a project
- eating a meal together
- role playing in a group
- playing a board game

Moral/spiritual and aesthetic development: through socialisation, children develop a set of values and codes of behaviour and an awareness of beauty in the environment; for example, look for a child or children

- playing a game with rules
- gardening
- listening to music
- looking at paintings
- enjoying an outing, and following the rules of safety
- helping with a display

Sensory development: development of the five senses of sight, hearing, taste, touch and smell; for example, look for a child or children

- smelling cakes cooking
- eating food they have cooked
- playing with clay, water and sand
- painting
- taking part in a musical activity
- looking at books

Many people have attempted to chart and record expected normal development, following observations of a large sample of children over long periods of time. It is important that you understand that there is a range and sequence of normal development and that not all children acquire skills according to 'the book'. For example, in possibly the most used book, Mary Sheridan's *Children's Developmental Progress from Birth to Five Years*, children are shown as walking

Cooking helps sensory development

alone at 15 months, whereas many of you will know children who walk much earlier than this. This could be because Sheridan's work was done mainly with children in the 1950s, when many children were confined to cots and playpens for a longer period of time than children today, for whom there is greater emphasis on stimulation and play. Some children may show accelerated development in one area, whilst remaining on a plateau in another. For example, a child who is speaking in sentences at 18 months may, at the same time, have difficulty in coordination.

One of the reasons for fully understanding normal development is to make you aware of development outside the norm and whether such development is advanced or delayed. This can only be detected through detailed objective observations.

Observing a child's interests and strengths allows the staff in the establishment to plan activities that will extend further development and add to the child's enjoyment and stimulation.

In Appendix 1 we have devised a broad outline of normal development to help you with your observations. This is by no means the definitive text in this area and you will need to do a great deal of reading and be advised by your tutors so as to gain a full understanding.

A Practical Guide to Child Observation and Assessment

Understanding children's needs

All animals have basic needs. Children, as human animals, are no exception.

It is important that you understand the needs of children and become sensitive and perceptive in meeting these needs or in assisting parents to do so.

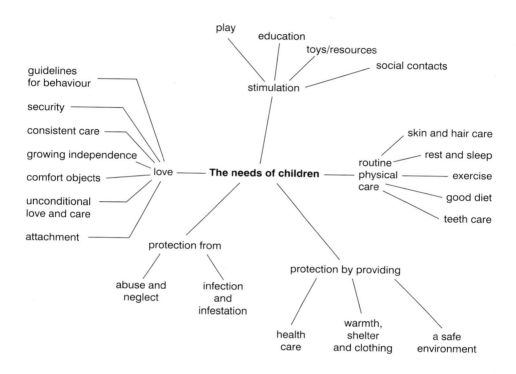

By recording objective observations you learn in a practical way how to become aware of these needs and how to meet them. For example, your observation of a child who drinks a great deal of milk in the placement, whilst often rejecting their dinner, might prompt your supervisor to discuss this with the child's parents. At another time you might record a child who is reluctant to use the outside play area. This could lead to you finding out the cause of this and helping the child to overcome their fears.

Attachment between a mother and her newborn baby

Children's needs

Love	Children need to receive affection and to form close relationships. Without emotional security, children find it hard to make loving relationships in later life.
Food	Children need an appropriate healthy, balanced diet to ensure optimum growth and development.
Shelter	Children need to be sheltered from a hostile environment, to be adequately housed, to be suitably clothed and to be kept safe from injury, abuse and disease.
Stimulation	Children need the opportunity to play, to move around freely with safety so as to explore the environment and learn from their experiences.

Activity

The table above shows children's basic needs.

What else do you think children might have a right to?

What is the difference between needs and rights?

Social interaction with children and adults

Promoting good social relationships is an important part of the childcare and education practitioner's role. It will start with supporting the bonding between baby and mother right through to sorting out peer-group rivalry among seven-year-olds. It is only by closely recording the social interactions which are taking place that you gain an understanding of children's needs in this area and become able to help them establish good relationships. It is often revealing to watch how a new child will try to integrate herself into an already established group. A child who is skilled socially will wait on the perimeter of the group until she is invited to take part. A child who does not have these skills may demand to be allowed to play and push herself forward, where she will quite often be rejected. By observing the socially skilled child it is possible to teach these skills to those children who find it difficult to make friends.

By observing children's rapport with the adults in the team you will see what is good practice, and this will help you to establish your own relationships with children.

Changes in behaviour

Systematic recording of observations will enable you to identify behaviour patterns and allow you to see behavioural changes in a child. For example, you might find that a child appears more independent than before, or acts more thoughtfully towards one of their peer group. Observing these positive behavioural changes might allow you to understand what had brought this change about, and build on this when planning activities and routines.

Careful observations are useful to monitor negative changes in behaviour, when a child suddenly regresses to less mature conduct, as the change in

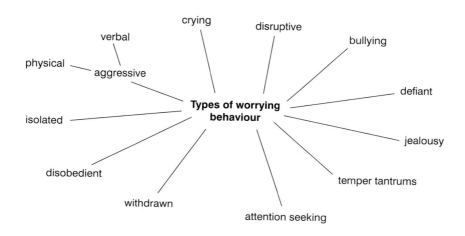

behaviour might have a physical cause, such as the onset of illness, or it might be an emotional response to family problems or changes. Sometimes some element in the setting can upset a child, and practitioners need to be aware of their own behaviour and responses to others.

You need to understand that all children are individuals and will behave and react differently in similar situations. Through detailed observation, you will be able to predict individual behaviour and reactions to situations, for example understanding that one child would be fearless on a new climbing frame whilst another would hold back. You should respect both reactions.

Healthcare and safety

Making sure that children have the freedom to explore their environment with safety is part of your role as a childcare and education practitioner. Observations will make you aware of any potential hazards in the children's immediate environment and allow you to protect them from danger. This will link in with your growing awareness of developmental stages, for example stairs, which are a hazard to a crawling baby, yet present a challenge to a toddler. Your observations and knowledge of children's healthcare needs will alert you to signs of ill health.

Illness is obvious if a child suddenly vomits or has a skin rash. A child who appears more lethargic than usual will come to your notice through your routine

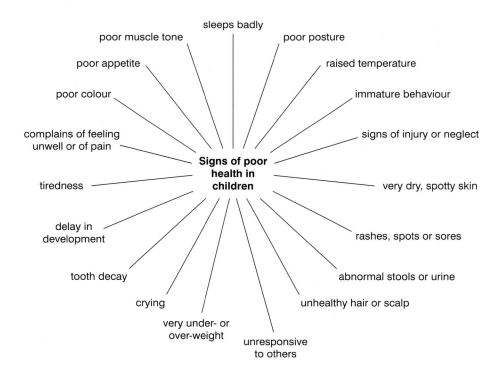

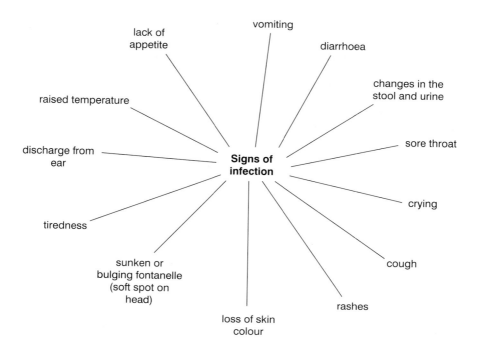

vomiting

lack of appetite

diarrhoea

raised temperature

changes in the stool and urine

discharge from ear

Signs of infection

sore throat

crying

tiredness

cough

sunken or bulging fontanelle (soft spot on head)

rashes

loss of skin colour

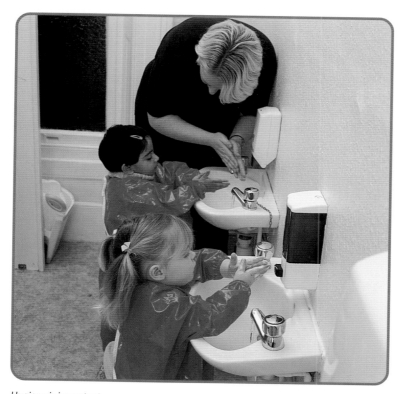

Hygiene is important

observations of a normally lively active child. Several observations of a child who appears to have health problems will lead you to discuss them with your supervisor, who will talk to the parents, perhaps resulting in referral to another agency. All parents will hold a personal health record for their child that records details of the child's growth, development, immunisations and any major health problems.

Activity

Look through the accident record book in your placement.

In your opinion, were any of these accidents avoidable?

Is there a particular area where accidents occur frequently?

Record keeping and future planning

All establishments are now expected to keep detailed records and assessments of the children in their care, and you should see many different examples of how this is achieved. Observations will provide information for other members of staff and other professional workers such as speech therapists, social workers and educational psychologists. They may be used with parents to share accurate information in a professional way.

Observations are never an end in themselves, but should be used to promote and extend children's development, fulfil any needs which are not being met, support children in establishing meaningful relationships, acknowledge and understand changes in behaviour, and ensure a safe, happy and healthy environment. Identifying any concerns should lead to assessment and possible action either individually or as a staff team, and may lead to discussion and planning with parents. The rules of confidentiality will ensure that any information is not passed on to others unless it is in the child's best interest to do so.

3 How to observe children

Learning outcomes

Through observations you learn to identify good practice and become aware of your own role in seeing how childcare and education practitioners meet the needs of children from many different backgrounds and establish good relationships with their families. The placement will benefit from your observations in the planning and reviewing of their practice. You will not only observe individual children but, by looking at groups of children, you will see different patterns of behaviour and the interactions of the individuals within the groups.

Your tutors will help you with structuring your observations and make clear what is expected of you.

Beginning the process

The time has come for you to write your first observation. One way of preparing yourself for this is to carry out the following activity. Having done this, you will be aware of the complexity of carrying out clear objective observations on children. Do not be despondent; the more observations you do, the easier it will become. Your completed file will demonstrate the progress you have made.

Activity

With a friend, visit a playground, local park, or supermarket – in fact, any place where you are sure to see children – and, having gained permission from the parent or caregiver, separately record one child's activity and behaviour for five minutes. After completion, discuss the following points with your friend.

- How did you feel? Anxious, silly, unsure of what onlookers may have thought, or detached and objective, or any other feelings?
- Were you trying to write too much, recording language, physical movements and emotional responses?
- Did other adults interrupt and distract you?
- Did the child stay in the same place for the allotted time?
- Did you have to move?
- Was it obvious what gender the child was?
- Were you aware of the home language?
- Approximately how old was the child?
- Was the child aware of you?
- Did you ask the parent or caregiver's permission first?
- Did you have enough paper?
- Did your pen run out of ink?
- Could you write quickly enough?
- Did your account of the child's activity agree with that of your friend?
- Were you able to make sense of what you had recorded?

Guidance from your centre

At the start of your training, your tutor will help you to prepare for recording your first observations. Throughout your training, you will look at different techniques and methods of assessment and your observations will contribute to the overall learning of the group. In addition to this, your tutor may well use some tutorial time to give personal advice.

Your collection of observations will be regularly submitted and assessed. As with all the new subject areas to which you are being introduced, you will become more knowledgeable and skilled as your training progresses.

Children can learn from the outdoor environment

Supervision in the placement

The person who is responsible for you in the workplace should be made aware of the number and range of observations you are required to carry out. It is your responsibility at the start of each placement to talk to your supervisor or assessor and discuss what observations and activities you need to record during your time there. You might find it difficult to find enough time to do your observations if there is more than one student in the placement or there are staff shortages, in which case planning is essential.

The supervisor has the following responsibilities:

1 Inducting you into the placement routines and making you aware of the timetabling of events, both daily and weekly. This will help you to plan the best time to do your observations.
2 Giving you opportunities to get to know the children, and giving you the time to answer any questions you might have about them. You will need the dates of birth of all the children to put on your observations.
3 Agreeing times during the week when you will not be expected to take part in the placement activities so that you can do your observations, making sure that all the staff in the room know what you are attempting, so that you are less likely to be interrupted.

4 Advising parents that observations are being carried out by students, and obtaining their permission.

5 Reading your observations and signing that they are a true account of what took place. Nursery and school staff frequently have many demands made on them. Despite this, most supervisors and assessors find the time to discuss and comment on your work and help you to interpret what you have seen. This should help you to develop skills and techniques and allow you to understand the progress you are making.

As a student you will need to find out the general policy and procedures used by the staff to observe and assess children in their care so that you can enrich and add to their own file of assessments. This is often a useful time to ask for their equal opportunities policy, which you will need to study and adhere to. The placement will have rules and guidelines regarding confidentiality and data protection, which you must fully understand before you start any observations.

Involving parents

The establishment will have informed all the children's parents that you will be writing observations about the children, governed by the rules of confidentiality. All parents have the right to be involved in decisions affecting their child's care and education, and have access to their child's records, unless there is a legal restriction that prevents it.

As you become more skilled, and with the approval of your supervisor, it is good practice occasionally to share these observations with the parents. They might be able to help you understand the child better, to point out why their child behaved in an atypical fashion, and to make you more conversant with the child's cultural and social background. It would be quite impossible to do some types of observations, such as a child study, without the help of the parent. It is enlightening for the parents to see how someone outside the family views the child and her needs and achievements. It is not necessary for students to take photographs or record videos of the children for their portfolio as this may breach the rules of confidentiality and the rights of the children.

Involving parents will help you to assess the validity of your observations and interpretation: for example, a child who does not have the confidence to read in class might well be reading fluently at home, whilst enjoying a cuddle with her parent.

Always remember that the parent knows the child best. Establishing a good relationship with the family can only be in the best interests of the child. It is now universally considered good practice to involve parents in all aspects of the child's development and educational achievements, and all reports and assessments have to be available on request. This undoubtedly has led to more objective record keeping.

Starting out

Make sure that this is a convenient time for the rest of the placement team for you to attempt your first observation. As an observer, you will need to blend into the background, so as not to spoil the results of your observation. Avoid making eye contact with the children and any adults who might be involved in your observation. Sit as still as you can and avoid making unnecessary noises, such as rustling paper. Try not to appear involved in what you are observing, but look as if you are purely concentrating on your notetaking.

Very few observations need the presence of an adult (particularly the observer) to interact with the child. You are there to study children's behaviour, needs and development. Occasionally, interaction with an adult makes an interesting observation, but only if it demonstrates something particular about the child.

Decide to observe a child who, as far as you know, is well within the normal range of development and behaviour. Note down the date of birth, first name, and length of time the child has attended the establishment. Taking a pen or pencil and a notebook, place yourself in an inconspicuous part of the area, where you have a good view of the child and/or activity you wish to observe, and where you can hear what the child is saying. Avoiding eye contact, concentrate solely on the child,

Recording an observation

rather than describing in detail the activity. If other children come up to you and ask what you are doing, just explain that you are doing some writing for your tutor. If a child needs help with a task, direct her to someone else, if possible. If you find yourself becoming involved in an activity, stop your observation and try again later. If there is an emergency, when a child might be at risk, you must of course stop what you are doing and deal with it.

When you have completed your observations, you should spend two or three minutes reading them through to make sure they make sense and that you have all the information you need. You will then be able to write them up outside of placement time, feeling confident that you have completed a full record.

General guidance

Always keep a pencil or biro and a notebook in your pocket so that you are ready to record anything of interest that occurs. When you do your first observations, you will be well advised to look at one child, doing one activity, for a short time. As you become more skilled, you will use a variety of different techniques and be able to look at groups of children, which will help you to assess social interactions and relationships.

Observations will also fall into various categories. Some observations that you do will be unplanned. An event will occur that you find interesting or that demonstrates an aspect of development that you wish to record, for example a distressed child parting from a parent. Others will be planned by you; for example, your centre might require you to set up an activity so that you can record a child's manipulative skills with scissors. These observations will be of fairly short duration and you may or may not record that child again. You may also be asked to observe a child over a longer period of time, perhaps looking at several areas of development. These are called longitudinal observations or child studies. Occasionally, you may be required to record a quick impression of a child at a particular time, such as when she first joins a nursery group. This is sometimes called a snapshot observation and is also useful as a preliminary start to a series of observations on one child.

Many courses will ask for specific information, and this can be usefully done by having a common front page (see page 30).

The front page

You will need to include the following information on a front page.

Number and date of observation

These are important for two reasons. Firstly, you may be asked to present your observation portfolio to the moderators in date order, so that they can see a progression in your work. Secondly, you may forget to make a note of the age of the child or children you are observing. This will be easy to look up in the records if you record the date. The observation number is inserted in the box at the top left-hand corner of the page.

Method

Here you will note the technique you are using to record the observation, such as a written record, a checklist or a time sample, etc. These are explained in the next chapter. Information may sometimes be presented in a more understandable way by the use of tapes, charts or other media, but you will need to justify their inclusion. Your tutors will give you guidance on this.

Type of setting

This refers to the actual place where the observation is recorded, for example the nursery class. Remember not to record the name of the establishment. On occasion, it might be illuminating to describe the wider context of the setting; for example, a rural nursery school might have a different philosophy from that of an inner urban nursery class.

Immediate environment

This would indicate exactly where the recording took place, for example the book corner. If you were recording language, it would usually be very different in the book corner from that used in the playground.

Times

Noting the length of time of the observation is important for the reader's understanding of the event. The time of day might also be important. For example, a child crying for a parent would have a different meaning early in the morning than at dinner time, as it is not unusual for some children to protest when separating from their parent. On the other hand, it would cause more concern if it happened later in the day, possibly suggesting illness or a reaction to a problem at home or in the establishment. If children are introduced to a new activity, it is usually found that they can understand it more easily when they are not tired, so the time of day might influence a child's response.

Number of children and adults in setting

The reason you are asked to record this is to help you to evaluate your observation. For example, a child fiddling with her hair, isolated in the corner of the room, would show more worrying behaviour than if this were happening at story time in a large group and with an adult present. The impact of other children and adults on an observation obviously has a large influence. The role of the adult or adults present might be relevant to the observation. For example, the headteacher walking into the room might have a different impact than a parent.

Observation ☐

Date:

Method:

Start time: Finish time:

Number of children present:

Number and role of adults present:

Permission sought from:

Type of setting:

Immediate environment:

First name(s)/initial(s) of child(ren) observed:

Brief description of child(ren) observed:

Ages:

Gender:

Aim of observation:

Signature of supervisor:

Note that the box, top right, is used for recording the number of reference of your observation.
You may photocopy this sheet for your own use. © *Nelson Thornes Ltd.*

A Practical Guide to Child Observation and Assessment

First name(s)/initial(s) of child(ren) being observed

As a student, you should use only the first name of the child, or the initials. It would be a breach of confidentiality if you record the whole name. It is permissible to use a false name. For the same reason, you should never name placement staff or parents, but put 'the teacher', 'the childcare practitioner' or the 'parent'. Obviously, the name of the placement should never appear on your observations.

Brief description of child(ren) observed

You might like to add something here that is relevant to your aim or evaluation of the observation. For example, the length of time the child has been attending the setting, the health of the child, problems with settling in to the establishment and so on.

Age(s)

Anyone reading your observation will want to know how old the subject is so that they can assess if the child is immature or advanced from the behaviour described. Years and months are usually written as follows: 2 years, 1 month = 2:1.

Gender

Knowing if the child is male or female may be relevant to your evaluation. For example, identifying that wheeled equipment in the play area is dominated by the boys may lead the placement to discriminate positively to encourage the girls to have a turn first.

Aim of observation

You need to state the aim of your observation. This may be to look at, for example, a particular area of development, a healthcare routine or perhaps a part of the early years curriculum and the reason why you are observing this area.

The following are three examples of aims:

- To observe and assess language development in a child of 14 months, to plan how best to extend her language
- To observe a baby's physical development by using a checklist devised by the student, to assess the baby's gross and fine motor skills
- To observe and record aggressive behaviour in a four-year-old over a period of one week, using an event sampling technique, so as to assess if any attacks were provoked by other children, or if there was any cause in the environment to upset the child.

It is important to spell out clearly both your aim and the reason for it, as this will underpin the evaluation and interpretation of the observation.

If something occurs that you find interesting and you record it, you will need to explain why you are including it. For example, there may be an argument over sharing equipment and to your surprise the older child gives way and bursts into tears. You may go on to discover that the child is incubating chickenpox, demonstrating how behaviour might change in an unwell child.

Signatures

To verify that your observation is a true and accurate account, you will need to obtain the signatures of your supervisor and/or the parent. These may appear on the front page or at the end of the observation.

The observation

The following page or pages will then contain the recording of your observation, whatever method or technique you have decided is appropriate. Finally, you will need to interpret your data. This is the part that most students find very difficult at first, but the value of doing an observation is to show what you have learnt from what you have observed, and to be able to use it to benefit the child.

Interpretation

When you have finished your observations you need to interpret what you have seen and heard. On many courses you will be expected to record the following.

General comments/background information

Before you begin to interpret your observation, you may wish to inform your reader of relevant background information. The length of time that a child has attended the establishment can have an important effect on her behaviour. If a child has only recently started at the nursery, note the date of arrival in your comment. It takes some children quite a while to settle into a new environment. The position of the child in the family may be relevant. Eldest children may be more used to adults, but more reluctant to leave the parent. Youngest children may be used to having their wishes anticipated for them by other members of the family and find it difficult to be independent. If the language of the child at home is different from that of the establishment, the child might find life very confusing at first, and become frustrated and unable to express her needs. This could lead to aggression, crying or withdrawn behaviour.

It may be necessary to comment on the weather. Children who have been kept in all day because of driving rain may not behave in as cheerful a fashion as a group that has run around in the fresh air for some time. An unusual activity may have been set up by the establishment. It might be necessary to describe this briefly to ensure understanding of your observation.

Evaluation and assessment

A good way to start is to look at the aim of the observation and begin to link the evaluation with this. You must not make assumptions using words like 'I think' or 'perhaps'. Only comment on what you have actually seen. Reporting what your supervisors or other people might tell you about the child or the family background is not usually relevant to the observation, but if you are sure that it is you put 'Following discussion with the supervisor/parent . . .' and then write what you have been told. Beware of making judgements based on race, disability or gender stereotypes. The gender of the child may be relevant, but be careful not to express sexist attitudes: you should not be surprised if a girl enjoys rough play, or a boy wants to spend time quietly in the home corner. Not all black children will be tall for their age or advanced in locomotion skills. A child with a physical disability may be advanced in cognitive development.

Assess the child's/children's skills, for example in the use of toys and equipment, language and behaviour in relation to their age. Are those skills within the normal range, advanced, or immature? (You should consult various books on child development and information from your centre, together with the charts in Appendix 1 on the different ages and developmental norms; make comparisons with other children of the same age; and discuss any difficulties with your placement supervisor or assessor.)

If the observation is of a child behaving in an unusual way, for example being very aggressive or anxious, upset or clinging, note whether this is typical of that child or very unusual. You or your supervisor may be able to suggest a possible reason for the behaviour.

Remember to be objective, never repeating hearsay, making unsupported value judgements, labelling children or being influenced by prior knowledge. Never personalise comments, for example making comparisons with your own children, other children in the establishment or children well known to you.

You may find that you have not achieved your aim. This is acceptable if you explain why the aim has not been met.

Possible referral/recommendations

This is where you can show that you understand the reason why observations are important.

Owing to your observation, it may become clear to your supervisor or line manager that some action may need to be taken to satisfy the needs of the child you have observed. For example, the child may have a possible hearing loss and should be referred for medical assessment. You might discover that another child can read quite fluently and not even the parent was fully aware of this. More appropriate encouragement and stimulus can then be provided. If you discover that girls in the nursery rarely use the large blocks, you can create a situation to encourage them in this area of play, which is valuable for their spatial and planning skills. You will be able to assess the value of the activity to the child.

Describe three different ways that this photograph might be interpreted.

Personal learning

You may well be able to demonstrate that the theory of childcare and education learnt in your centre has been observed in the practical setting. You might decide to follow this by doing another observation, perhaps using another technique. You may wish to repeat the activity to reinforce learning skills, varying part of the activity to promote a different outcome. You may also learn something about yourself and your attitudes. For example, you may consider a child to be very aggressive, and feel pleased if the child is absent on occasion. Once you have done a detailed observation, you might discover that the child is often provoked into fighting, possibly being teased about living in a non-traditional household or wearing inadequate clothing. This may lead you to spend more time with the child, to consider ways of getting him to cope more appropriately with his feelings and to reassess your initial attitude.

As you assess what you have learnt from recording an observation, the effectiveness and value of what you are doing will become clear. You will become aware of what is good practice and of the professional skills you will need when you are qualified.

References and bibliography

Whilst writing your interpretation, it is necessary to indicate what has helped you to evaluate what you have observed. Whilst recording observations is a practical skill, it would not be possible for you to carry this out without some underpinning knowledge and understanding. You should relate the behaviour/development that you have observed to known influential factors about child development put forward by theorists. For example, the observation may show a child behaving in an immature way. You may be able to relate this to a recent hospital admission, and will need to provide a reference to support their statement that a hospital stay can cause regressive behaviour. A child may have extreme difficulty in settling into the establishment, and you would refer to one of the theorists known for their work on bonding and emotional development.

 ## Activity

You will need to refer to child development theorists in your interpretation. Some of the most distinguished are

- Piaget
- Bowlby
- Bandura
- Gesell
- Bruner
- Vygotsky
- Chomsky.

In what particular areas were they most interested?

Name six other child development theorists, and their area of work. Discuss your choice within your group.

References would include textbooks, websites, magazine and newspaper articles, and college material. Any references given in your observation need to be cited in the body of the work. All quotes from publications must be shown with quotations marks and show the author and the year of publication. If you fail to do this you may be accused of plagiarism.

Having completed your observation you need to list all the references you cited in a bibliography in alphabetical order of author (see page 184). A bibliography is a list of all the sources you have consulted during your interpretation, whether or not you have used them as a reference within the text. To compile a bibliography you list the authors alphabetically, by surname, followed by the first name or initial, the year of publication, the title and the publisher.

Before requesting students to record observations of children in their training placements many centres use the Child Development and Observation tapes developed by Siren flms. These videos show children in everyday settings providing realistic situations for students to observe. The tapes show various observation techniques and cover a full age range.

4 Commonly used observation techniques

Learning outcomes

There are many proven techniques used in observing children. Depending on the reason for your observation you will find some methods will relay the information more clearly than others, and in this chapter we discuss the most commonly used techniques. As a student, you will be expected to use a range of techniques to demonstrate your competence in observing and assessing children.

The written record

When you first start observing children, you will most likely use the method referred to as a written record. This is the commonest type of observation technique, and may be used to record a naturally occurring event (free description), or a structured recording, where a specific task is set, appropriate to the age and stage of development of the child. You will probably use this technique several times before embarking on any other method. It is a description of an event unfolding in front of you, written in the present tense so that your reader can appreciate what is happening more easily.

Advantages

- You are using a skill which you practise every day and that is familiar to other people.
- Only a notebook, watch and a pen or pencil are required.
- It can be carried out when convenient to all, with little preparation and no formal planning.

Disadvantages

- You may not be able to convey all you wish as the events are happening very quickly.
- It is sometimes difficult to keep up with all that is happening. A form of shorthand or a code might be useful.
- Inexperienced observers might find themselves recording something that is not relevant to the observation.
- The piece may be repetitive and boring, and could be conveyed better using a different technique.
- It may produce an unwieldy amount of information.

Examples of written records are shown on pages 39–49.

Associative play

Observation [7]

Physical development

Date: 6.11.03

Method: Free description

Start time: 11:00   Finish time: 11:20

Number of children present: Whole class

Number and role of adults present: 1 teacher, 1 student

Permission sought from: Supervisor

Type of setting:

　　　Infant school

Immediate environment:

　　　Hall setting, piano in top left corner, canteen to the right.

First name(s)/initial(s) of child(ren) observed: K

Brief description of child(ren) observed:

Ages: 5:7

Gender: Male

Aim of observation:

　　　To observe a child's large physical development in relation
　　　to norms of development.

Example 1 of a written record.

Observation: Physical development

It is a dark and rainy morning. All the children are standing in the hall. The teacher explains that there are five different activities, and each group will be on a certain activity for a while and then will swap. K is standing still, with both arms by his side. The teacher asks the children to jump around the hall and to freeze when she blows the whistle. Taking off from his right foot, K is jumping in a clockwise direction, both feet together. He is waving both hands in the air beside him. The whistle blows and K stops suddenly. The teacher then asks the children to jump sideways. Bouncing on the tip of his feet, hands clenched, he bounces along the floor in a sidewards direction. The whistle blows, and with his knees bending slightly he puts out his right foot and uses this to balance upon. Standing still he turns his body to the left, knees together. The teacher calls out the different colour groups and the children all move to their first activity. When the yellow group is called K walks slowly, taking large steps.

K sits in the middle of a blue hoop, with his knees bent upwards. His hands are resting on his knees. Standing up on his right foot first he reaches for a bat with his right hand. He clasps the bat tightly with both hands. Suddenly he jumps forward on his right foot and stops just in front of the box. He leans down towards the box and reaches for a ball. Placing the ball in his left hand and the bat in his right he drops the ball onto the floor. He is crouched over close to the ball, knees bent, feet wide apart. Using his right arm he moves the bat with short, quick movements to try and hit the ball with his bat. The ball goes out of the hoop. Putting his left foot forward first he runs quickly to the corner of the hall, where the ball is situated. He takes the ball and walks quickly back to the hoop. He sits down, legs crossed, both hands holding the bat.

The teacher stops the children and tells them to move on to activity 2. K skips sidewards to the skipping ropes and reaches down to take one. He swings the rope backwards but it hits the heel of his left foot. He bends down to touch his heel with his right hand. K is finding this activity difficult and is unable to jump over the rope. He tries to jump up and down, his hands holding onto the rope. The whistle blows and K moves on to the next activity.

Taking small, quick steps, he walks to the top right corner of the hall. With his left hand he picks up a beanbag, steps into the middle of a hoop and moves the beanbag into both hands. He throws it high into the air, head facing upwards. He places out both hands and catches the beanbag. He is smiling and throws the bag into the air, again by using both hands. He tries to catch the bag with just his right hand – his fingers are widely spread apart and he is using quick, small arm movements to try and catch the bag. In trying to catch the bag he takes a small step backwards to regain his balance. He fails to catch the object and the bag goes out of the hoop. He takes a small jump out of the hoop, taking off his right foot and landing on his left first. He bends down from his waist and picks up the object with his knees slightly bending. He walks back to the hoop and is about to throw the bag into the air, when the teacher stops the children and asks them to sit down. He sits down quickly and crosses his legs, placing his right leg over his left.

The teacher then asks the children to point to the next activity they are moving on to. K understands what the teacher has said and responds by looking at the next activity, instead of pointing.

He gets up and walks slowly over to the next activity. He has to kick a ball around a cone. Using both feet, he kicks the ball slowly around the cone. He stops, and puts his right hand up to his head. He scratches his head and then places his arm by his side. He kicks the ball again, and it rolls to the side of the hall. He walks over and takes his ball. He sees his friend has lost his ball under the piano and helps him look for it. He goes down onto both knees, landing on his left first. He rubs his right knee and places both arms on the floor. He begins to lie down to look under the piano, his arm stretched out with the cheek of his face near the floor. His friend finds the ball, so K stands up, walks back to his cone and drops the ball next to it. His right foot goes forward and he curls it around the ball. He kicks the ball slowly, moving his right foot forward. He stands on the ball, trying to control it.

Example 1 of a written record (continued).

After being on the activity for a few minutes, K runs on to the last activity. He reaches down towards the floor and takes a ball with his right hand. With his feet wide apart, he stands outside the hoop. He drops the ball and it bounces on the floor. With his fingers spread wide apart, he tries to clap his hands together before the ball comes up. He manages to do this, but fails to catch the ball. The ball rolls to the side of him. He gets the ball and returns back to his hoop. He drops the ball again, but this time he manages to catch the ball with both hands. K is smiling. He places his right foot, then his left into the hoop and then kneels down on his right knee first. 'Quick' he says to his friend. The teacher stops the children, but K continues to bounce the ball, whilst sitting down on the floor. The children are then asked how they feel about doing physical education. K raises his right arm into the air, but places it down again when someone else answers.

Interpretation

The aim of this observation was to observe a 'child's large physical development in relation to the norms of development', over an unlimited period of time. The child was observed for 20 minutes during a physical education session. The child participated in five different activities (for a few minutes on each), which were set up around the hall. The equipment provided varied for each activity. For activity 1 there were hoops, bats, balls; for activity 2 there were skipping ropes; for activity 3 there were hoops, beanbags; for activity 4 there were balls, cones; and for activity 5 there were balls and hoops.

Physical development is the 'growth, development and control of bodily movements' (Beaver et al., 2001, p. 361). There are two main areas to physical development:

1 Gross motor skills: whole-body movements, e.g. kicking/catching a ball, running
2 Fine motor skills: manipulative skills, e.g. writing, completing jigsaws; hand–eye coordination.

Throughout the five different activities the child would have been developing hand–eye coordination, for example, in activity 1, balance; in activity 2, about textures and properties of different objects, e.g. the rough texture of the skipping rope, compared to the softness of the ball. K would be gaining the ability to respond to commands and instructions as well as improving upon his listening and concentration skills. The child would be developing fine-motor skills, i.e. holding the bat, grasping the skipping rope, as well as improving his physical development.

Physical development plays a large role in a child's overall development. As a result of this, children should always have the opportunity to participate in physical activities. Physical activities give children the chance to learn new skills. A child will want to explore its environment and will need physical skills to do this. Once a child has learned a skill, the child can build upon this skill and develop it further. This will also affect a child's confidence, independence and self-esteem. Physical skills develop from participating in physical exercise and from repetition.

Physical education has many positive effects on a child, so it is important not to discourage children from participating and to praise the children. As well as keeping children healthy and building their strength and physical skills, it can promote a child's social and emotional development. Children are perhaps able to release their emotions and feelings during physical education, helping them to feel happier within themselves.

K shows good control and good concentration skills. At age 5 K shows normal physical development. He showed good balance and coordination skills – playing ball games, hitting ball with bat. K showed a preference for particular activities and this is of normal development (Meggitt et al. 2000, p. 88). He appeared to be more confident and happier with activities which involved catching objects, rather than other activities, such as skipping, in which he was unsure, and kicking the ball around the cone, which he found difficult. However, the ability to kick a football and catch and throw balls with accuracy is not usually developed fully until 6 years.

Example 1 of a written record (continued).

As stated by Sharman et al. (2001), children aged 5 should have developed the skill to skip, but K found this activity difficult and struggled to do it. This could show that he is behind development in this area. This could be improved by providing him with more activities which will help his balance and coordination. As well as this he will need support, praise and guidance. Many children at this age have difficulties with balance and this should be recognised, with appropriate equipment provided. Children are continuously improving their physical skills. One way in which a child's skills of movement and balance could be developed further would be to play 'Follow My Leader'. This activity could be useful for K. The teacher would set out various pieces of equipment, such as hoops, ball, beams. The children would follow the teacher around the equipment and stop when the teacher stops.

K showed a good understanding of rules. He was able to follow the rules, and saw them as being unchangeable. This could be linked to Piaget's theory of moral development, as stated in Flanagan (1996, p. 95). K would be in the Moral Realism stage. K would follow the rules of others and the rules must not be broken. If a rule was broken K would evaluate it in terms of consequences.

Personal learning

I feel that the method I used (free description) for this observation worked well. It enabled me to focus directly on K and make a detailed account of his physical skills during a physical education lesson. I feel the activities K participated in enabled me to achieve a detailed picture. One problem I encountered while using this method was that I found it hard to get all the detail needed because the events were happening quickly. One way this could be solved would be to video the child during a physical education lesson. Although this would provide me with the chance to look at the child in more depth I feel it would be unnecessary because the child's behaviour would change. It would be necessary to gain permission from the supervisor and parent.

Physical education sessions enable a child to improve upon physical skills. Physical education can also help a child's self-esteem, confidence and independence, as once a child has achieved a particular activity they will want to practise and improve upon that skill. From this observation I observed how it is also important to question children about how they are feeling during physical education, as this will not only help their vocabulary and communication skills, it will also help the child to recognise what happens to themselves during physical activities.

It is necessary to remember that all children are individuals, and as a result every child will progress at a different rate. While one child may be able to kick with accuracy already, another may be struggling with this, finding it difficult, and losing confidence and self-esteem. Children who are struggling may require extra support and help. As a result of this, lessons must be planned carefully to ensure that all children have the chance to improve their skills and that they don't feel left out if they are unable to complete a certain activity. Teachers must provide the child with support and encouragement and make sure that the tasks set are to the child's developmental level.

I have learned how it is important to allow the child to play independently as well as to play with others (cooperative play). This will encourage the child to improve their confidence and independence as well as encouraging them to work in a team and to communicate with others (as a result improving social skills).

Recommendations

K has only been attending Year 1 since September 2003 so it is vital that all the activities he participates in during lessons help to develop new and existing skills.

It would also be necessary for K to have a repetition of activities to enable him to practise and understand key skills and concepts.

I would promote K's development by providing him with a wide range of different activities during physical education as well as providing extra support for activities he finds

Example 1 of a written record (continued).

difficult. This could be implemented by the teacher demonstrating how to do each activity. This would help children who are struggling to see what movements the teacher makes, and from watching the teacher they will be able to copy the actions and will feel more confident at participating in the activity. This was suggested by Bandura, who developed the Social Learning theory (Flanagan, 1996). This theory proposed that a child who watches someone and copies their behaviour is learning from someone. The child is more likely to imitate the behaviour of people who are powerful and caring, and this is shown within the teaching environment: for example, if a child is rewarded for behaving well, other children are likely to copy this behaviour because they have seen someone being rewarded.

Staff at the school could promote K's physical development by providing regular opportunities for physical exercise, providing appropriate equipment, such as stilts and beams to encourage balance and coordination. Teachers should allow the children to become involved in different sports/activities, and lessons should be structured to incorporate this and help the children improve their physical skills.

Bibliography

Beaver M. et al. 2001, *Babies and Young Children*, Nelson Thornes.
Flanagan C., 1996, *Applying Psychology to Early Child Development*, Hodder & Stoughton.
Meggitt C. and Sunderland G., 2000, *Child Development: An Illustrated Guide*, Heinemann.
Sharman C. et al., 2001, *Observing Children: A Practical Guide*, 2nd edition, Cassell.
Tassoni P. et al., 2000, *Planning Play and the Early Years*, Heinemann.

Supervisor's signature

K. Jones

Example 1 of a written record (continued).

National Curriculum (numeracy)

Date: 7.3.03

Method: Free description

Start time: 9:30   Finish time: 10:20

Number of children present: Whole class

Number and role of adults present: 1 teacher, 1 student

Permission sought from: Supervisor

Type of setting:

Infant school

Immediate environment:

Class environment. There are 6 round tables, carpet area to the right, computers to the left of the class.

First name(s)/initial(s) of child(ren) observed: F

Brief description of child(ren) observed:

Ages: 6:0

Gender: Male

Aim of observation:

To observe a child involved in a task from one of the aspects of numeracy in the National Curriculum and assess the child's level of understanding.

Example 2 of a written record.

Observation: National Curriculum (Numeracy)

All the class are sitting on the carpet facing the teacher in the top right corner. F is sitting to the left of the teacher with his legs and arms crossed. His head is raised and he is concentrating on what the teacher is saying. The teacher begins the maths activity by completing several mental problems. The teacher counts forwards and backwards in ones from 10 to 30. F appears quite confident in this and happily joins in the activity. Next the teacher counts in tens starting from different numbers. She begins on 2 and continues, 2, 12, 22, 32. F joins in, speaking clearly and loudly. The teacher then counts backwards. F doesn't expect this and at first continues to count forward. He quickly understands and continues to count backwards. This activity is then repeated from 6, 16, 26, 36, 46. F, who is still sitting still, legs crossed, listens to the pattern and soon joins in.

The teacher then explains that for their main activity they will be looking at partition of two digits. She asks if any one knows what partition means. While several of the children raise their arms, F appears unsure about what the question means and sits quietly on the carpet. One child explains that partition is where you split a number up into tens and units. The teacher uses the whiteboard to show some examples and asks the children some simple questions to begin with. F occasionally raises his right arm to answer a question and is keen to answer. After showing a few examples the teacher uses partition cards and asks the children how many tens and units there are in certain numbers. The first example is 71. F doesn't raise his arm, instead he waits for someone else to answer. F remains focused throughout. Once the children have a grasp of tens and units the teacher moves onto hundreds, tens and units. The teacher asks varying questions to different children using different numbers, depending on the development and understanding of the child. F is keen to answer and gets his question right. F's face is happy and he is sitting up straight with his legs crossed and his arms resting on his knees.

The teacher gets the class's attention by moving her hands and fingers while the children copy. F does this eagerly. The teacher explains to two groups, the cylinders and the cones, what they will be doing, and sends these children to their tables. F stands up slowly, and walks over to his table taking small steps. He pulls out his chair with both hands and sits down. In front of F there is a tray of pencils and a selection of number cards laid out on the table. The aim of the activity is for children to choose a card and write in their books the number of tens and units. Once this is completed children take another card.

F leans forward and chooses 77. He places this down in front of him using his right hand. F is unsure about what to do next. He puts up his arm and says 'What do I do, I don't understand'. The teacher explains to F using an example. He reaches for a pencil and in his book he writes 77 =. He is unsure about how to complete his answer. His left arm is holding his book in place and he moves his right arm up to his forehead. After referring to the previous example he slowly finishes his answer: 77 = 7 tens + 7 units. He checks his answer and then continues with the next.

He puts the card down in the pile and reaches for another. Again F is unsure of what to do and needs guidance. After completing several cards with assistance he attempts to work independently. He gets his answer right and he begins to become more confident. He works steadily through his work; he is taking his time and is thinking carefully about every answer he puts. The teacher rings the tambourine and all the class stop what they are doing and put their arms into the air. It is clear that F has heard the tambourine but continues to work through the teacher's next instructions. F is concentrating on his work.

The teacher asks all children to put their work into a neat pile on the table, to get a number fan from a box in the back of the classroom and then sit down on the carpet. F now quickly finishes his last question and goes to get a number fan. The aim of the number fan is for the teacher to ask a question, e.g. 'How many tens are there in 54?' and then the child will find the answer on the fan. The teacher begins with smaller numbers. She starts with asking the children how many tens are in 32. F seems unsure about what the answer is and looks to his

Example 2 of a written record (continued).

friend for help. F holds up the same answer as his friend and it is the right answer. The teacher repeats this with numbers of varying difficulty. F looks puzzled by this and begins to become disruptive. He looks at his friend's answer and bases his answer on this. It is now snack time and the teacher stops the class and asks all the children to put their number fans away and go and get milk. F is the last person off the carpet and walks slowly over to the milk.

Interpretation

The aim of this observation is to observe a child involved in a task from one of the aspects of numeracy in the National Curriculum and to assess the child's level of understanding. Maths includes five different aspects. These are numeracy, shape, sets and sorting, pattern, and measuring. This observation focuses on numeracy. 'Numeracy includes counting, estimating, recording numbers' (Beaver et al., 2001, p. 384), as well as addition, subtraction, division and multiplication.

As Matusiak (1992, p. 91) says, 'Maths is about relationships of number, size and shape. Children need to explore these in a meaningful way so that they develop a fascination for maths'.

Maths plays a vital role in children's life as it is used every day. Children get dressed by putting on clothes in a certain order (matching, sorting), laying the table (matching, counting), going to school/bed (number, time). Maths can help develop children's problem-solving skills and logical thinking. To help develop reasoning and logic skills I would recommend that adults use open-ended questions which will encourage children to think independently and explain their ideas behind their reasoning, e.g. 'Why doesn't it work?', 'What will happen if . . .?'

Throughout this maths activity the teacher played an active role, particularly at the beginning and end of the activity. She encouraged all children to participate, by asking different children questions.

It was necessary for the teacher to explain hundreds, tens and units. She implemented this by talking to the children, using a variety of teaching methods and by doing work on the board, for example:

Hundreds	Tens	Units
2	7	1

Maths is reflected in the Year 1 classroom through the use of symbols, displays and appropriate materials. There is a large number line hanging from end to end of the classroom, and small number lines on every table. There is a large hundred square on the carpet which is visible to all children. The maths equipment is easily accessible and children are encouraged to use this equipment to help solve mathematical problems. There are several maths displays with the maths symbols on them. This will encourage children to become familiar with how maths language can be used as symbols, e.g. Add +. As Beaver et al. (2001, p. 403) note, 'As they develop an understanding of number, children will begin to recognise numerals and use symbols to record their work'.

The language which F used could help adults see if he had understood the activity. Language development 'is the development of communication skills' (Meggitt and Sunderland, 2000, p. 2). At age 6 F showed good language development. He was able to use appropriate vocabulary, e.g. tens, units, bigger, add, equals. He had a good pronunciation of his words and he spoke clearly. As stated in Meggitt and Sunderland (2001, p. 96), children aged 6 should be able to 'talk fluently and with confidence'. F was able to do this and was of normal development for his age. Although F didn't communicate much with peers he was able to communicate effectively with adults.

F was able to follow instructions. He listened attentively to the teacher and did what was asked. This could be linked to Piaget's theory of moral development which proposed that children aged 5–9 would be in the Moral Realism stage. Rules and instructions at

Example 2 of a written record (continued).

this age are unchangeable and as a result children would follow the rules of others (Flanagan, 1996, p. 95).

F remained focused throughout the maths activities and concentrated well on the main activity in particular. F showed normal development, as children aged 6 should be able to concentrate for longer periods of time (Beaver et al., 2001, p. 121), and was able to persevere with the activity even when he was struggling at the beginning. By the end of the activity his confidence had improved and he was able to work independently without any support. From this I have learned how after initially helping children with a problem and ensuring they understand the key aspects, children can benefit from working on their own, solving problems for themselves and then having higher self-esteem which will encourage them to learn.

As stated in 'A Parent's Guide to the Primary Curriculum', by age 7 children will be able to 'count on or back in ones or tens from different starting numbers' and to 'count, read and write whole numbers up to 100'. F was able to do this confidently and had a firm understanding of counting numbers 1–100. He recognised all the numbers and was able to distinguish which numbers were higher than others.

In the National Numeracy Strategy it suggests that by the end of Year 1 children should be able to 'solve simple mathematical problems; learn to recognise and predict'. F successfully predicted number patterns in the mental maths activity, particularly on the counting aspect. The NNS also suggests that children should be able to 'organise information in simple ways. Discuss and explain results'. F organised his work in columns which made it easier for him to see patterns and follow previous examples.

Throughout this maths activity F showed good understanding of numeracy. He worked hard at solving the problem when he struggled and succeeded. He had a firm grasp of partition and by the end of the activity was able to explain what he had learnt and explain which number is the tens number and which is the units number.

All the children in this activity would be learning how to talk about, recognise and recreate number patterns. Children would be learning counting skills and how to split numbers into hundreds, tens and units.

Personal learning

For this observation I feel the method I used (free description) wasn't as effective as other methods. Although it enabled me to look in depth at one child I found it was difficult to look at all aspects of a child's development in detail. I feel it would be more effective to use several checklists, e.g. language, emotional, to assess a child's level of understanding. This would provide me with several detailed checklists of the child which could then be combined to get a true picture of the child's understanding.

From completing this observation I have learned about the importance of working with other staff in order to meet the requirements of the National Curriculum. The National Curriculum is a framework given to teachers by government. It is important to communicate and work alongside others as this will ensure that all children are taught in a similar way and that similar teaching methods are being used. The maths lesson in Year 1 was in three main parts:

- Mental maths: 10 minutes (an introduction to partition of two digits)
- Main activity: 30 minutes
- Plenary: 10 minutes (summary of what has been learned).

I feel this worked effectively for the children as it helped children to grasp the main ideas.

I have learned about how children should also experience maths through having first-hand experiences of these activities. This will help children to 'develop confidence and understanding in the subject' (Beaver et al., 2001, p. 401).

J. Bruner proposed three stages of learning and suggested that children should be actively involved in their learning and that by having these experiences it helps the child to 'develop their ideas and thinking' (Tassoni et al., p. 26). Bruner also believed that children need to be

Example 2 of a written record (continued).

reminded of past experiences. He called this iconic thinking. From looking at Bruner I have learned how activities should be linked to past experiences, as children will be familiar with these and as a result the activities will be of interest and will encourage children to learn. Children will be able to link past skills with developing skills.

Froebel suggested that 'Adults need to provide the right environment and activities' (Tassoni et al., 2000, p. 16). Froebel's theory proposed that children should have adequate opportunities to experience things for themselves. Froebel encouraged practical work and through this children will learn about themselves, their environment and the world/society they live in. This will include showing appropriate behaviours for different situations, following rules and expectations, sharing, working and communicating effectively with others. From this I have learned how it is often more effective to allow children to work independently as this will encourage confidence, independence and problem-solving skills which could then be linked onto other areas of the National Curriculum such as science, where problem-solving skills are essential.

Children need to hear and see adults using maths for everyday purposes, for example the calendar, and counting attendance. This enables children to recognise maths and see how to use it appropriately.

I have learned about the importance of listening to children's questions as this will show how much they understand and what their interests are. From this, appropriate activities can be planned according to children's interests, as activities which encourage and motivate children to learn are essential to a child's development. Adults should 'model and encourage use of mathematical language' by, for example, asking questions such as, 'How many saucepans will fit on the shelf?' (Foundation Stage Profile, p. 75). By asking questions children will be encouraged to think behind their decisions and try out new ideas.

Recommendations

To help develop children's skills in mathematics at Key Stage 1 I would recommend that staff regularly repeat main topics, ideas and activities to ensure that all children understand the main concepts, as all children develop at different rates and this needs to be taken into account when planning activities. Staff at the school should use 'everyday experiences to reinforce mathematical learning', for example counting stairs, number of windows (Beaver et al., p. 404).

Children should be provided with first-hand experiences which will encourage learning. This could be implemented by planning a simple trip around the school counting objects; children could go a shape hunt looking for different shapes by counting the number of sides and corners and recording this information.

However, individual needs need to be taken into account, and activities should be planned to accommodate all needs; for example, a visually impaired child could be provided with alternatives which allow the child to use other senses but still learn the main objectives for that lesson.

The framework for teaching maths suggests that staff should use stories, rhymes and songs to promote 'learning across the curriculum', by linking one area of development to another; for example, through playing with dough children would be learning mathematical language such as 'more' and 'less', and they could recreate patterns they have observed by activities such as making numbers out of dough. Dough can also be linked onto science as children would be learning about different properties, textures, weights of the dough.

To help promote numeracy children could count and touch or move objects. This would help children to understand that numbers also have meanings instead of just being numbers. Staff could encourage children to predict before counting. Activities such as guessing the number of crisps in a beaker at snack time could help promote this.

Staff need to observe children's progress as they develop and make any alterations if necessary. This will ensure that work set is developmentally appropriate and will also encourage children to move on to the next step in their development. In this activity the

Example 2 of a written record (continued).

A Practical Guide to Child Observation and Assessment

teacher altered the questions she asked particular children, and planned different main activities depending on the child's ability. This was to accommodate every child's needs and to ensure that adequate support could be given if necessary.

I would recommend that staff use a variety of teaching methods to help teach mathematical concepts to children. Number rhymes such as 'One two three four five, once I caught a fish alive' and 'Ten green bottles' will provide a new, exciting way of learning for children. Children should be able to regularly play mathematical games such as 'Snakes and Ladders', as they will need to use a dice and counters, and the games involve taking turns and sharing. Children should be encouraged to help adults when money, measuring or counting is involved. Children could participate in simple cooking activities which will help promote weighing, measuring, timing and counting skills. Other methods may include the computer, sand and water trays, working on small tasks in groups, and class activities. Children should be encouraged to record their work in a variety of different ways, such as graphs, tally charts and lists. In the three main parts of the maths lesson the teacher used different methods to interest and encourage children to participate:

- Mental maths: talking to children, whiteboard, partition cards
- Main activity: number cards.
- Plenary: number fans.

Therefore I would recommend that the class and outdoor environment reflect mathematics and that it is applied in all areas. This could be implemented for example in the role-play area by providing money and scales, which will encourage counting, estimating, number, weighing skills.

Sand, water trays and counters can all be used to help promote numeracy and maths development. Children could be encouraged to estimate how many beakers it takes to fill objects, to make comparisons of size and volume which will also teach children about quantity and mass. Sand and water can also be linked to other areas of the National Curriculum and help promote children's development.

Bibliography

A Learning Journey: A Parent's Guide to the Primary School Curriculum, 2002, Department for Education and Skills.
Beaver M. et al., 2001, Babies and Young Children, Diploma in Child Care and Education, Nelson Thornes.
Flanagan C., 1996, Applying Psychology to Early Child Development, Hodder & Stoughton.
Foundation Stage Profile, 2002, Qualifications and Curriculum Authority.
Matusiak C., 1992, Foundations for the Early Years, Scholastic.
Meggitt C. and Sunderland G., 2000, Child Development: An Illustrated Guide, Heinemann.
Tassoni P. et al., 2000, Planning Play and the Early Years, Heinemann.

Supervisor's signature

P. Murray

Example 2 of a written record (continued).

Time and event samples

Time samples

Time samples are exactly that: a sample of time when you observe a child over a fairly long period. For example, you might choose to watch a child for one minute, from the time she arrives at the establishment, at 10-minute intervals, until home time. Preferably, you would try to do the samples at least once more in the same week. Children can show different behaviour early in the week, or early in the day, than they may do later on.

Time samples may also be used to find out how children are using the toys and equipment in the placement. This is often helpful to the staff, who might think that all the equipment is being used equally, and then discover that some pieces of equipment are more popular than others. This could lead to enlarging or extending some areas of play.

It is a good idea to attempt a time sample on a child about whom there is some concern. Before you start, describe the concern in some detail.

The following are examples of possible concerns:

- withdrawn behaviour
- shyness
- inability to relate to others (children or adults)
- extreme lethargy.

Ask your supervisor or line manager if there is a child causing concern and why. Observe the child closely for a day or so before starting the time sample. Write down in full all the problems the child seems to be facing. Completing a time sample (see page 51) will show you whether there is a real problem which needs intervention or referral, or whether, on the other hand, the concerns are not as worrying as was first thought.

Event samples

An event sample (see page 69) is used to record events during as long a period as possible, and at least for a week. The events you are looking out for may be displays of aggressive behaviour or lack of self-control. You would record these events each time they occurred, noting down the time of day, the duration of the event, whether they were provoked or not, and a comment on the seriousness of the behaviour. The aggressive behaviour might include:

- hitting and fighting
- biting
- spitting
- scratching
- extreme verbal abuse
- disruptive behaviour (such as destroying equipment or interfering with activities)
- temper tantrums.

Time sample

Concern:　　　　　　Home language:

Time	Social group	Activity and language	Emotional effect

You might also find it useful to use event samples to chart the behaviour of children who are unhappy. You may be looking for:

- frequent outbursts of crying
- extreme comfort behaviour, such as rocking, sucking and masturbation
- clinging to adults.

Some areas of healthcare can be recorded using event samples. For example, a child who frequently leaves the classroom to use the lavatory during the day may have a urinary tract infection.

As in a time sample, try to observe the child first for a day or so, and then write down as fully as possible the perceived problem. You might find that the child reacts only when provoked by other children, or when tired or hungry. It is easy to presume that one child is the root cause of all disturbances. (Staff have been known to shout out a child's name when observing a fight and then discover that the child was absent that day.)

Time and event samples are used in establishments to detect if children have a real behaviour problem or if it is just the perception of the staff. If the samples show that the child needs help, these sorts of observations can be presented to professional colleagues. Sometimes these observations are used in case conferences where the child is being discussed by a team of professional people. If the problem is not as serious as was first thought, the sample might show the staff that the way the child is being managed may be contributing in some way to the child's distress. The sample will enable the whole team to sit down together and see how the child can be helped in the establishment to resolve a temporary anxiety.

Advantages of time and event samples

- A collection of precise data.
- More closely focused.
- When completed, data is readily accessible.
- Easily understood by other professionals and parents.
- Professional appearance and format.
- Can reveal unsuspected patterns of behaviour.

Disadvantages of time and event samples

- Allocating the time to complete the task: some time and event samples might need to take place over long periods of time.
- The expected behaviour may not appear during the time the child is being observed.
- Remembering the time when doing time samples.
- Keeping one child in sight at all times, without making it obvious to the child that he is being observed.
- After the first session, the child may be absent for some time.
- The observer might lose concentration and miss a recording.

Baby learning a new skill

Date: 25–28 September 2003

Method:

Time sample. As I will be observing a new skill that is being developed, the time sample will enable me to do this effectively, at regular intervals – therefore noticing any developments made.

Start time: 2:40 (25.9.03)   Finish time: 12.55 (28.9.03)

Number of children present: 1 (10)

Number and role of adults present:

0 (6). There are 7 adults present, these being the four childcare practitioners, the supervisor, myself and a visiting parent.

Permission sought from: Supervisor

Type of setting:

The nursery is privately run. It is situated near a busy high street, yet the surrounding area is relatively quiet with semi-detached houses on the opposite street. There is also a zebra crossing close to the nursery, ensuring safety for those who use it.

Immediate environment:

At the moment, there is a new/visiting parent with her baby in the room. Two of the babies are in the 'sit 'n' swing' chairs, some of the babies play with the plastic cars on the floor, while others are playing with the sorting containers laid out – two of the babies do so, while supported by a floor cushion. The room is quiet.

Example 1 of a time sample.

First name(s)/initial(s) of child(ren) observed: T

Brief description of child(ren) observed:

Ages: 7 months

Gender: Female

- T has been attending the nursery for six weeks.
- Both her parents are British.
- She has no sisters or brothers.
- She is generally in good health.

T has only been attending the nursery for six weeks, yet she seems to have settled in very well. Her favourite pastime in the nursery has to be the (hanging) bouncer – which she stands/jumps in whilst continuously smiling! Until very recently, she could only lie down or sit up with the help of support cushions; she is now sitting unaided, for longer periods, which means she is reaching for and exploring more objects using both hands. She is a very contented baby, who will play for long periods without crying or seeking the attention of adults.

Aim of observation:

The aim of this task is to observe a baby learning a new skill, which is the baby learning/gaining the confidence to sit up, unaided. I will also consider safety and the environment.

I want to carry out this observation in order to see the stage of development T is now at, and compare it with others of a similar age. Having interpreted the information, it may also be used in discussion with parents/carers, which can in turn help when planning further activities for the babies in the setting (particularly those of a similar age).

Example 1 of a time sample. (continued).

Date	Time	Description of activity
25.9.03	2:40pm	T is in the large tray filled with shredded paper. She sits up with the support cushion that she is fully leaning against. While in this position, she manages to play with/grasp a teething toy with both hands.
	3:40pm	T is in the carpeted area, lying down (supine position), as she holds a toy cube in front of her – using both hands. The cube falls and T tries to pick it up off her tummy. After a few moments, she stops and stares at the ceiling.
	4:40pm	T is in the 'Swing 'n' Sleep' chair, as a new activity has been set up on the carpet. I sit down with her in between my lap, but not helping her to sit upright – for the first time I have seen her do this! After two minutes she falls back onto me.
26.9.03	10:55am	Lies down with shaker in mouth. Childcare practioner sits her up, alone – which she achieves for two minutes – then slowly tilts to the right whilst still holding shaker, which has slid under her right arm. She cannot get a grasp of it with hands, so lies back down and sucks her thumb.
	11:55am	T recently finished her lunch and is lying on the large red cushion. She raises her head off the cushion – her face is strained as she stays in that position, she does not go any further, deciding to lie back down.
	12:55pm	Lies supine, as she watches supervisor shaking a tambourine (with hand). She reaches out her hands and passes it to T – who takes it by the handle and shakes it. It then falls to her side (on the left); for a few moments she tries to pick it up – succeeds! Now resumes shaking it.
	1:55pm	I am on my lunchbreak, and therefore unable to observe.
	2:55pm	T is playing with the shape sorter container on the carpet, while 'propped up' against the cushion. I remove this, while sitting behind her, which she copes with before tilting – to get her back upright, I have to prop her up with the cushion again, which she holds and sits upright.
	3:55pm	T has fallen asleep in the 'Swing 'n' Sleep' chair.
27.9.03	11:55am	T is sitting up unaided as she plays with a soft toy stacking ring. Four minutes have passed and she hasn't fallen back. Her facial expressions are calm – when she sees me looking at her, she smiles, while still holding the toy in her left hand.
	12:55pm	T, myself and the other babies are sitting/playing in the carpeted area. She reaches out and grabs my right index finger tightly, with both hands, to pull herself up, but doesn't manage so this time the child practitioner informs me that T is actually doing a poo!
	1:55pm	T is lying down and smiling, as she flaps her arms up and down quite rapidly. Of her own accord, she attempts to get up from this position – raises her head and legs in the process. Cannot manage it and her head drops back down.
	2:55pm	T is sitting up as she grasps a 'wipe clean' strawberry soft toy with both hands, while sucking it.
28.9.03	10:55am	T is sitting unaided, but with a support cushion behind her. She reaches out and holds a large red car, while still balancing. After four minutes, she leans back on the cushion.
	11:55am	T and three other babies are sitting in the large sand tray. She sits comfortably, as she sifts the sand through her right hand and plays with the rake with her left. After five minutes she leans back on the low-rise wall.
	12:55pm	T sits upright without help or support, but soon after falls back, and immediately starts to cry. I reassure her, saying 'You should be happy for what you just did T!' She stops crying.

Observation
Time sample
Interpretation

As stated, T is seven months old. With regard to her physical development, she should be able to do the following (Minett, 1994, p. 129):

- 'Sit upright for a short while on the floor, with her hands forward for support
- Use straight arms to lift her head and chest off the ground
- Take her own weight on her legs when being held, and enjoy bouncing up and down'

I can say that T has reached each of these stages, as over the few days that I observed her, she showed competency in all of the above.

For example, on 25 September, T showed two aspects of the above behaviour – as she sat upright, she also managed to grasp and hold a teething toy with both hands. T also loves to spend time in the (hanging) bouncer, in which she frequently puts pressure on her feet for long periods of time without tiring. Although T does not yet crawl, the time spent in the bouncer may even build her confidence, as she is *making* something happen for herself; as Hurst and Joseph (1988, p. 30) state, 'the self-confidence that one can achieve new understanding and skill and the perseverance to keep trying, form powerful dispositions towards achievement'.

So, the more opportunity T has to consolidate/build on her newly attained skills, the faster she can move on to the next stage of development. On one occasion, T managed to sit up without any help, but she soon after fell back; as I was beside her, I immediately offered comfort and a cuddle, which stopped her crying. I feel it is important that the adult makes the baby feel secure at times like this; she did still make progress and it should be recognised and nurtured. As Tassoni and Beith (1999, p. 177) state: 'Children need to be encouraged and praised. One of the best ways to help children's self-esteem is to provide them with a positive atmosphere, which will make children feel special, noticed and valued. Children need to feel that they can fail and not be criticised.'

T also managed to reach out and grasp objects as she sat upright, unaided on many occasions. At one point she dropped the toy at her side and, after a few moments, succeeded in picking it back up, which I was pleased to see, as she didn't give up until she had the toy in her hand again. As stated by Meredith and Gee (1987, p. 12), 'At seven months, a baby will watch a toy being dropped (if it falls out of sight, they forget about it). They can also pick up objects with either hand, using the palmar grasp, and *transfer* it from one hand to the other.'

By the end of the observation, I noticed that T was sitting up by herself, for longer periods. This may be because she had more opportunities to practise this new skill, which will inevitably improve her competency at it. Throughout this observation, I also found that T developed a way to raise her body off the floor – by raising her head and legs, which worked! So, it seems that using this 'trial and error' method is an effective way to acquire new skills. Beaver and Brewster (1994, p. 137) say:

> Trial and error learning is the earliest stage in development. The infant is trying out solutions to a problem in a random way and will try and fail, try and fail, until they arrive at a solution. This will probably involve returning to the problem many times. Trial and error can be very frustrating for the infant and careful intervention is needed to suggest ways forward for her.

I also agree that these can be frustrating times for the baby, as T often got upset, having not achieved what she wanted – to sit up from the supine position. However, with the help of a supportive adult, this can be overcome, with the wanted result being achieved.

Meeting of stated aim

I can say that I *have* met my aim – that is to observe a baby learning a new skill. I have also looked at safety within the environment.

Example 1 of a time sample. (continued).

Evaluation of selected method

I feel satisfied with the time sample method. This method allowed me to observe T at intervals, over a period of a few days – which proved effective in tracking how she *progressed* during this time. It also enabled me to devise my own intervals at which I observed, which I found easy to follow.

Other advantages include the following, as listed by Hobart and Frankel (2000, p. 63):

- A collection of precise data.
- More closely focused.
- When completed, data is readily accessible.
- Easily understood by other professionals and parents/carers.
- Professional appearance and format!

However, as with all methods this too has its disadvantages. I felt that the format did not allow me to include as much information as I would have liked. Also, any spontaneous behaviour that occurs while I am not observing cannot be included, yet it may be of great relevance to the task. I also found it awkward to observe T and keep a track of the time too.

Beaty (1998, p. 20) also outlines some disadvantages:

- It does not describe the behaviour, its causes or results because it is more concerned with the time.
- It is limited to observable behaviours that occur frequently.
- It is not an open method and therefore may miss much important behaviour.
- It does not keep units of behaviour intact because its principle concern is the time factor, not the behaviour.

There are, of course, alternative methods to be used. For example, the written method would have proved effective, as it would allow me to record the behaviour as it unfolded, including spontaneous behaviour of relevance. Not having to keep my eye on the time while observing would give me the freedom to focus on T's behaviour.

Other advantages include the following, as listed by Tassoni and Beith (1999, p. 92):

- Both structured and naturalistic observations can be carried out.
- Provides open data that can be interpreted later.
- Only a pen and paper is needed.

With permission of the supervisor and parents, a video recording of the observation would have proved very useful, as much more information would have been included, which other professionals could look at as it unfolds on film (particularly helpful if a developmental delay is noticed). As Beaty (1998, p. 30) states, 'Videotapes make it possible to record live child action for later observation and discussion with staff members. They are especially useful for discussion with members of staff who may not have witnessed the behavioural incident you observed.' I think this is of great relevance, as inviting those to watch the tape who were not present at the time allows for a more objective overview of the behaviour observed.

I feel that I observed T in an objective manner. There is little point in observing infants if the observer has any preconceptions of the infant – be they positive or negative. Observations are carried out in order to help children progress in all areas of their development, or to identify any particular needs. This will only be achieved if the observer has a truly impartial attitude. Tassoni and Beith (1999, p. 89) say: 'If we have pre-conceived ideas about what a child is like, we are more likely to look and record the behaviour we expect, rather than the actual behaviour. To make it as accurate as possible, we must be careful that any prejudices and stereotyped ideas are stripped away.'

Recommendations

Having observed T, I feel that she is indeed at her age/stage of development – including her learning a new skill.

Example 1 of a time sample. (continued).

In order to build upon her progress in sitting up by herself, the adult can perhaps try to get T to roll over from her front to back, which may lead to her crawling, in the near future. For as Meredith and Gee (1987, p. 44) state:

- By eight months, the baby should move around by rolling over and over.
- Can sit unsupported if she keeps still.
- Gets into crawling position, and rocks back and forwards, but cannot actually move along.

As there is a key worker system in my setting, I think it would be a good idea for the worker to spend some time in helping T to build upon her newly acquired skills and move her on to the next stage of development. I also noticed that T managed to reach out for and grasp many toys, which she held as she sat up unsupported. The worker could therefore build on her manipulative skills, by handing her two objects at once, so that she'll gradually learn not to drop the first but to hold one in each hand. Offering her toys at different angles will encourage her to work out how best to take them – which I think T will benefit from, as at one point I noticed that she tilted over to her right, whilst trying to grasp a toy in her hand.

As T becomes more mobile, the layout of the environment must be considered in terms of safety. The more mobile babies of this age are, the more dangerous their surroundings become, as they will be exploring them without awareness of the potential hazards. As Einon (1998, p. 21) says:

> A consequence of the speed with which an immobile baby becomes a sitting, rocking and crawling one is a constant need to update safety arrangements. While a child is immobile you can leave a hot drink on the table . . . once the child can move you have to be more careful. Don't wait until she shows signs of crawling: most children can pivot across the room before they can crawl.

All of the above suggestions must of course be carried out in collaboration with the parents/carers, in order for the staff and parents to do their best for the infant and ensure that continuity of care and education is given. As Bruce and Meggitt (1999, p. 144) state: 'If the partnership between parents, staff and child is going to develop well, then each needs to trust and respect each other.'

Bibliography

Beaty J., 1998, *Observing the Development of the Young Child*, Prentice Hall.
Beaver, M. et al. 1994, *Babies and Young Children, Book 1, Development 0–7*, Stanley Thornes.
Bruce T. and Meggitt C. 1999, *Childcare and Education*, Hodder & Stoughton.
Einon D, 1998, *Learning Early*, Marshall.
Hobart C. and Frankel J., 2000, *A Practical Guide to Working with Young Children*, Stanley Thornes.
Hurst V. and Joseph J., 1998, *Supporting Early Learning*, Open University Press.
Meredith S. and Gee R., 1987, *Entertaining and Educating Your Pre-school Child*, Usborne.
Minett P., 1994, *Childcare and Development*, John Murray.
Tassoni P. and Beith K., 1999, *Nursery Nursing*, Heinemann.

Supervisor's signature

G. Shaheen

Example 1 of a time sample. (continued).

Gender roles outside

Date: 10–12th May 2001

Method: Time sample

Start time: 10.50 Monday morning

Finish time: 11.40 Wednesday morning

Number of children present: Various numbers, ranging from 19 to 31

Number of adults present: 1–5

Permission sought from:

> Supervisor, who is the nursery class childcare practitioner in an inner-city primary school.

Type of setting:

> In a busy nursery in a multi-cultural area of London where there are tower blocks in the surrounding streets.

Immediate environment:

> Most of the children were playing outside in the nursery's play area. The area is shared by children from both nursery classes. The observation took place in various areas of the outside area, as the children were using the wheeled equipment and were moving in all directions.

Example 2 of a time sample.

Brief description of child(ren) observed:

Ages:

Various children were observed between the ages of 3 and 3:11.

Gender:

There were 16 girls and 15 boys on Monday morning, and 19 girls and 16 boys on Wednesday morning.

Aim of observation:

The aim of the observation is to observe the 3 to 3.11 year olds using the wheeled equipment in the nursery's outside play area and, by using a time sample, to note whether a boy or a girl is using the equipment. I want to see if any one sex is dominating the outside wheeled equipment and by using the results of the observation to recommend ways the nursery staff can help the inequality in the nursery, because it is important that both sexes have the opportunity to use all the equipment in the nursery.

Hobart and Frankel (1996) state 'it has been observed that boys tend to dominate outside play and use the equipment. Measures can be taken to redress the balance . . .'

Example 2 of a time sample (continued).

Bar chart showing the number of times boys and girls were observed using the wheeled equipment in the Monday morning session (top) and in the Wednesday morning session (below)

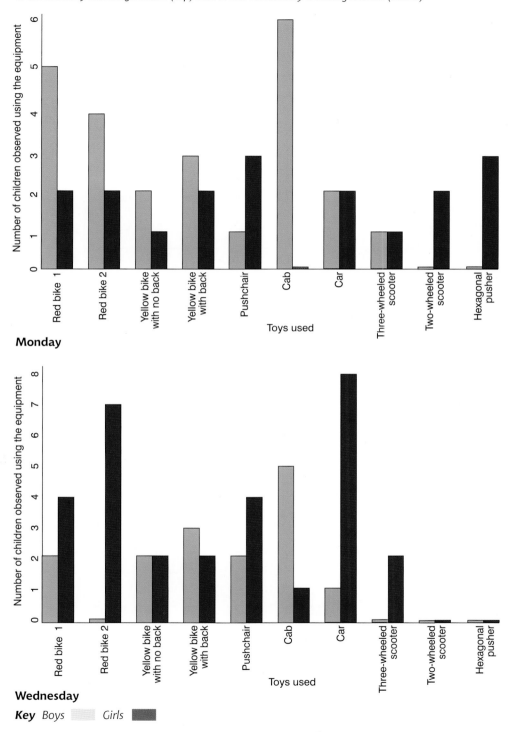

Monday

Wednesday

Key *Boys*   *Girls*

Time sample showing the results of the gender role observation

Time	Red bike 1		Red bike 2		Yellow bike with no back		Yellow bike with back		Pushchair		Cab		Car		Three-wheeled scooter		Two-wheeled scooter		Hexagonal pusher	
	M	F	M	F	M	F	M	F	M	F	M	F	M	F	M	F	M	F	M	F
Monday																				
10.50	1	0	1	0	0	0	1	0	0	0	1	0	1	0	0	1	0	0	0	0
11.00	1	0	1	0	0	1	0	1	0	1	1	0	0	2	0	0	0	1	0	2
11.10	1	0	0	1	1	0	0	1	0	0	1	0	0	0	0	0	0	1	0	0
11.20	1	1	0	1	1	0	1	0	1	1	1	0	0	0	0	0	0	0	0	1
11.30	0	1	1	0	0	0	0	0	0	1	1	0	1	0	0	0	0	0	0	0
11.40	1	0	1	0	0	0	1	0	0	0	1	0	0	0	1	0	0	0	0	0
Total	5	2	4	2	2	1	3	2	1	3	6	0	2	2	1	1	0	2	0	3
Wednesday																				
10.50	0	1	0	1	0	1	1	0	0	1	1	0	0	1	0	1	0	0	0	0
11.00	0	1	0	1	0	1	1	1	1	1	1	0	0	2	0	1	0	0	0	0
11.10	0	1	0	1	1	0	0	1	0	1	1	0	0	1	0	0	0	0	0	0
11.20	0	1	0	1	0	0	1	0	0	0	0	1	1	0	0	0	0	0	0	0
11.30	1	0	0	2	0	0	0	0	0	0	1	0	0	3	0	0	0	0	0	0
11.40	1	0	0	1	1	0	0	0	1	1	1	0	0	1	0	0	0	0	0	0
Total	2	4	0	7	2	2	3	2	2	4	5	1	1	8	0	2	0	0	0	0

Observation
Time sample: gender roles outside
Interpretation

Wheeled equipment can be used as an important part of the children's development as it can be used to develop balance, gross motor skills and spatial awareness. Therefore it is vital that both boys and girls get the opportunity to use the equipment. From the results of the observation, I can gather that the boys are perhaps dominating some of the wheeled equipment such as the cab as only one girl used it in the allocated time. It also appears that some toys are more popular with the children than others such as the hexagonal pusher and the two-wheeled scooter which don't get used much. The older children tended to use these toys, perhaps because there is more skill needed to manoeuvre them around the area. The results show that there is never a red bike free. This is because they are the newest of the bikes and the children say they go faster than the others. Both the boys and the girls like playing on these bikes. In the Monday session the boys were dominating the use of the red bikes but on Wednesday the girls were using them for most of the time. This may be because the boys preferred to play with some red balls, that had not been put out for a while, rather than the bikes for this particular day.

I found, through this observation, that the boys do use the pushchairs but they are mainly used by the girls.

Davenport (1994) states 'By this age children have developed a sense of gender . . . They often play in a "sex appropriate" way with "sex appropriate" toys.'

I came to the conclusion that boys and girls of this age can tell what equipment is generally associated with their gender. People at home may also influence them in playing with certain toys e.g. some of the boys may not experience pushing pushchairs at home if they have no sister or younger siblings. It may be the case that children need to be told that it is alright for the boys to play with dolls and to dress up, and for the girls to play with the construction kits, blocks and cars. From my own observations of the children, those with a sibling of the opposite sex are more likely to play with the toys which are traditionally associated with that sex. For example, a girl who has a brother is more likely to play with the cars, construction kits and other toys and vice versa, as they are used to playing with these toys at home.

Neaum and Tallack (1997) state 'This can result in boys and girls having a very limited view of choices available to males and females in our society.'

Personal learning

The time sample was a good way of carrying out this observation as it was easy to mark down whether a boy or girl was using the equipment. Hobart and Frankel (1999a) say 'Time samples may also be used to find out how children are using the toys and equipment in the placement. This is often helpful to the staff, who think that all the equipment is being used equally, and then discover that some pieces are more popular than others.' There are disadvantages in that the sample might not capture everything as I monitored the wheeled equipment only every ten minutes. The equipment might have been used by a child of the opposite sex in between the monitoring times. Using a barchart to display the results is a good way as you can clearly see which equipment is the most popular and whether it is used by boys or girls.

I have learnt through implementing this observation that what the theorists say about the boys dominating the outside equipment is true if I look at the specific results that I gathered by using the checklist.

Geraghty revised by O'Hagan (1997) says 'There is a large amount of research which shows that the early play experiences of girls are likely to result in them being less aware of space, less adept at large motor skills such as riding bicycles.'

I have learnt about the importance of both male and female children having the same opportunities to enhance and develop their skills. It is of equal importance that the boys are encouraged to take part in the quieter activities, as that the girls should be encouraged to take

Example 2 of a time sample (continued).

part in the physical activities. The nursery staff need to work as part of a team and decide how they are going to make sure equal opportunities is practised in the early years setting.

Geraghty revised by O'Hagan (1997) states 'If all children have equal access to all activities, with the staff giving equal encouragement to take part in these activities, than it must become a positive policy of the establishment rather than just left to the decision of each individual member of staff.'

Recommendations

The results from my observation show that the boys tend to dominate play with most of the wheeled equipment. I suggest that the time sample should be continued for a few more sessions to see whether these results are typical. If they are, then the balance of girls and boys needs to be equalised. There are several ways of doing this. The staff can separate the bikes into two groups, using one for the girls and one for the boys. Another way is to have a session where only the girls are allowed to use the bikes and another where only the boys are allowed to use them. I feel that this will bring to the children's attention that they are different and that people treat them differently and this could be a drawback.

I think the best way to deal with the problem is for the staff to let the girls go on the bikes more than the boys. I feel this would work because at the nursery where I am based the children come and ask for a go on the bikes, especially the red bikes, as they are the most popular of the wheeled toys. The children do this because they find it difficult sometimes to share the wheeled equipment. According to various authors children of this age still find it hard to share and take turns.

Physical activities should be supervised

Example 2 of a time sample (continued).

A Practical Guide to Child Observation and Assessment

Bibliography

Beaver M., Brewster J., Jones P., Keene A., Neaum S. and Tallack J., 1994, *Babies and Young Children, Book 1, Development 0–7*, Stanley Thornes (Publishers) Ltd.

Bruce T. and Meggitt C., 1996, *Child Care And Education*, Hodder & Stoughton.

Davenport G.C., 1994, *An Introduction To Child Development* (ch. 11, p. 168), Hodder & Stoughton.

Hobart C. and Frankel J., 1999a, *A Practical Guide to Child Observation and Assessment*, 2nd edition, Nelson Thornes.

Hobart C. and Frankel J., 1999b, *A Practical Guide to Activities for Young Children*, 2nd edition, Nelson Thornes.

Neaum S. and Tallack J., 1997, *Good Practice In Implementing The Pre-school Curriculum* (ch. 3, p. 40), Stanley Thornes.

O'Hagan M., 1997, *Geraghty's Caring for Children*, Ballière Tindall.

Sheridan M.D. revised and updated by Frost M. and Sharma A., 1997, *From Birth To Five Years, Children's Developmental Progress*, NFER–Nelson.

Woolfson R., 1997, *An A–Z Of Child Development* (p. 138), Souvenir Press.

Supervisor's signature

V. Riley

Example 2 of a time sample (continued).

Date: 4.9.01–8.9.01

Method: Event sample

Start time: Day 1   Finish time: Day 5

Number of children present: 40

Number of adults present: 9

Permission sought from: Supervisor and parent

Type of setting: Workplace nursery

Immediate environment:

Observed in all settings, both inside and outside the nursery.

First name(s)/initial(s) of child(ren) observed: G

Brief description of child(ren) observed:

Ages: 2:3

Gender: F

Aim of observation:

To assess behaviour of G who frequently bites both children and adults and displays aggressive behaviour such as punching and kicking.

Example of an event sample.

Event sample/frequency count

Concern: G frequently bites both adults and children. She is aggressive and demanding.

Home language: English

Day of week	No.	Duration	Provoked/ Unprovoked	Comments on seriousness
Monday	1	2 secs.	U.P.	G bit father as he left for work.
	2	1 min.	U.P.	Pushed A (1:9) over.
	3	2 secs.	U.P.	Bit E (2:3). Drew blood.
Tuesday	1	1/2 min.	U.P.	Hit C (3:0) with a wooden brick. Raised a bump on C's head.
	2	2 secs.	P.	Bit C (3:0) who pushed her over outside.
Wednesday	0			
Thursday	1	2 secs.	U.P.	Bit A (1:9). Not serious.
Friday	1	10 mins.	P.	G's father arrived 1/2 an hour late. G had a tantrum – inconsolable. She threw furniture around and attempted to bite nursery nurse.

Observation
Event sample: G
Interpretation

G's mother has left the family group of father and two older siblings. Her father has a demanding job, but does his utmost to bring and collect G on time. G's language is immature, she has difficulty in expressing her needs through speech.

Laishley (1987) suggests using an event sample to show clearly how often an unhappy child takes out her feelings of anger and frustration on other children. Because G's speech is poor, she often hits out rather than asking for what she wants. Biting is always a problem in a daycare group as the other parents, quite understandably, get angry when their child has been attacked. Therefore, it is important to try to deal with this as soon as possible. This is described in the College handout (1992).

G's behaviour is worse at the beginning of the week, after a weekend at home. She becomes calmer as the week goes on, and in between the aggressive episodes is a happy and industrious child.

Personal learning

From closely observing G this week I have learned that unhappiness can express itself in different ways in different children. I am going to discuss this observation at college, and I hope to get some suggestions as to how to stop G from biting and attacking other children.

I am pleased that I used an event sample to find out more about G's behaviour. This was an appropriate method to use and I shall continue to monitor her behaviour in this way.

Recommendations

The placement organiser has made arrangements to see G's father next Friday evening, when he has arranged to leave work early, to try to find out what G's behaviour is like at home and how it is dealt with. It is important for the nursery and the family to work together. The speech therapist has been asked to come in and assess G's language, as her inability to be understood is frustrating for her. Having two older brothers who understand her needs might make her less motivated to use words herself.

Bibliography

Laishley J., 1987, *Working with Young Children*, Edward Arnold.
College handout, 'The biter bit', 1992.

Supervisor's signature

K. Patel

Example of an event sample (continued).

Event sample/frequency count

Concern: Heritage language:

Day of week	No.	Duration	Provoked/ Unprovoked	Comments on seriousness

Checklists

Checklists or developmental guides are often used for assessing a child on one particular day, but can be used over a longer period. The placement might decide to do a 'snapshot' observation of all children within six weeks of entry to a nursery, or it might be used for a child about whom there is some concern.

Checklists can also be used for all the children in the establishment on a regular basis to enable the staff to plan for each child's needs.

They can be specific, looking at one area of development or assessing a child's behaviour, or they can be more general, covering all areas. There are some frequently used charts. Many placements will adapt or devise their own checklist. As an example, educational psychologist Hannah Mortimer has published a booklet containing 21 'playladders' (see pages 74–76). These are checklists of young children's activities in a variety of settings. They are a method of recording how a child plays at present, and they provide ideas on helping the child to reach the next stage.

Parents can be invited to share a booklet called *All About Me* written by Professor Sheila Wolfenden. This is a series of checklists which allows the parent to note down their child's development and progress from time to time (see the example on page 72). It is not tied to any particular age group. It encourages parents to record

- language development
- play and learning
- independence
- physical development
- health and habits
- social relationships and behaviour
- emotional development.

There is an opportunity at the end of the booklet to record concerns and to plan for the future.

You should have a good knowledge of the child before you attempt a checklist. Results may otherwise be distorted by the impact of an unfamiliar adult.

Activity

Using your library, find as many developmental guides, checklists and assessment schedules as you can.

Which professionals use checklists?

In what establishments are checklists used?

Snapshot observation

Name: Date:

Date of birth: Starting date:

Age:

	Describe
Home language	
Other language	
Place in family	
Physical description	
Physical skills	
Advanced in areas of development	
Social skills	
Toilet trained	
Language skills	
Delays in areas of development	

You may photocopy this sheet for your own use. © Nelson Thornes Ltd.

Now I can	Comments

build a bridge from three blocks
❏ yes   ❏ not yet

turn the pages of a book
❏ yes   ❏ not yet

turn taps off   and on
❏ yes   ❏ not yet   ❏ yes   ❏ not yet

fold paper   and fold clothes
❏ yes   ❏ not yet   ❏ yes   ❏ not yet

I am old enough now to

ride a tricycle   ride a bike
❏ yes   ❏ not yet   ❏ yes   ❏ not yet

unscrew tops off jars and bottles
❏ yes   ❏ not yet

thread beads   play with Lego   swim
❏ yes   ❏ not yet   ❏ yes   ❏ not yet   ❏ yes   ❏ not yet

prefer using my left or right hand
❏ yes   ❏ not yet

What else can I do?

What we already do at home to help my physical development

What we can do in future to help me develop my physical skills

Reproduced by kind permission of NES Arnold Ltd

Checklists often highlight areas of a child's development that have previously gone unnoticed. For example, a child who appears physically very competent may sometimes have difficulty in controlling wheeled toys. Being aware of this, the staff are then able to provide practice and encouragement. A child can also be shown to be mature in some way and this can be supported and extended.

After completing any checklist, you will need to write a summary, showing what you have learned and suggesting any possible course of action the placement might take to help or encourage the child.

Advantages

- A quick way of presenting a great deal of information.
- Results are obvious and readily understandable.
- Can be useful to combine with a longitudinal observation when carrying out a child study.
- Can be repeated to assess developmental progress.
- The same guide can be used for several children to find out more about the group. This can indicate gender differences – or show that there are none.
- Can be used by parents.

Disadvantages

- Care must be taken to maintain objectivity. It is tempting to put a tick against skills which you previously thought the child had achieved.
- Checklists may not show how competent the child is at the task, only that it has been completed.
- Checklists may not give a true picture if the child is less than cooperative on the day, or if the child is unwell.
- The child should be unaware of being assessed or may become stressed. You will have to show ingenuity to turn the assessment into a game as otherwise the data will be invalid and unreliable.

'Playladders' can be obtained by sending a cheque for £4.50 to QEd Publications, The ROM Building, Eastern Avenue, Lichfield WS13 6RN. Parts of the layout are illustrated in this handout.

Playladders

Playladders are checklists of young children's play as they go about their activities in nursery, playgroup or at home. They are a method of observing and recording how a child plays now, and they provide ideas on how to help the child reach the next step. 'Playladders' combine the step-by-step approach developed in special education, with the practicalities of what goes on in a busy playroom.

The Playladders booklet contains 21 playladders, each one representing an activity typically available for under fives, for example: climbing frames, painting, home corner, book corner or glue table. Each activity is broken down into progressive steps and skills. The emphasis is on flexibility, and users are encouraged to adapt, modify or add to the ladders to suit the particular child, culture and setting. There are also blank playladders to build up for yourself.

Playladders were originally designed for nursery and playgroup staff who had children with special educational needs in their classes.

Playladders provide the ideas for moving one step at a time from simple to more complex play, encouraging young children in their learning.

An example of the Playladders in use

Beth was a three-year-old who had just started at her local nursery class. At first, she was very quiet and spent the entire session walking up and down the room pushing a trolley. She resisted any advances from the adults and children. We used the Playladders to map her play; this needed a lot of help from her mother as Beth did so little for us in nursery. Together we concluded that Beth was still at an early stage in all areas of her play and social life, and that pushing a trolley was her safest option in her new and unfamiliar setting.

One of us began to befriend Beth, who gradually allowed the contact. She began to seek this helper out and would park her trolley for a moment while watching other children play, so long as the helper was nearby. She would help to clear up using her trolley and, in time, park it long enough to draw a scribble which she then carried around in it. Using the Playladders for ideas, and the trolley as a starting point, Beth gradually increased her repertoire of play and felt safe to leave her trolley and join in.

Postscript

If you don't work in a playgroup, but in some other kind of setting, don't be tempted to dismiss this format out of hand. It can readily be adapted for other settings. For example, during the trialling of the pack, this format was developed by a junior school teacher into a complete record-keeping system for children's progress in physical education.

Hannah Mortimer
Educational Psychologist
Stockton-on-Tees LEA

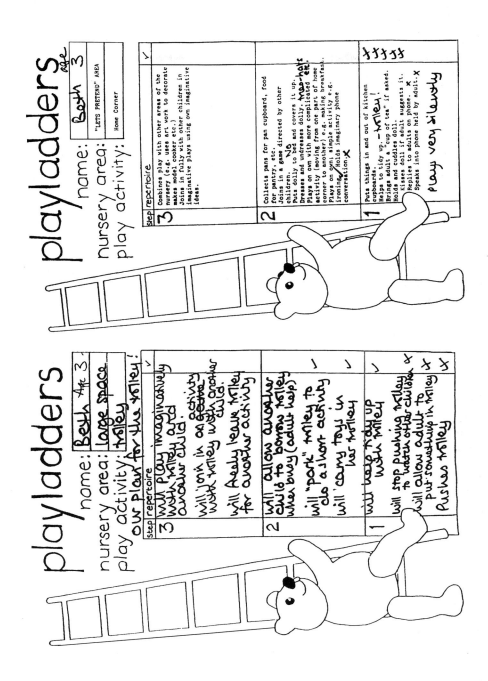

playladders

name: Beth age 3

nursery area: "LET'S PRETEND" AREA

play activity: Home Corner

step	repertoire	✓
3	Combines play with other areas of the nursery (e.g. uses art work to decorate, makes model cooker etc.) Joins in fully with other children in imaginative plays using own imaginative ideas.	✓
2	Collects pans for pan cupboard, food for pantry, etc. Joins in a game directed by other children. No Puts dolly to bed and covers it up. handbags Dresses and undresses dolly. etc. Plays on own with more complicated activity (moving from one part of home corner to another) e.g. making breakfast. Plays on own/simple activity e.g. ironing. Holds imaginary phone conversation. X	
1	Puts things in and out of kitchen cupboards/to tidy up. — trolley! Helps to tidy up. trolley! Brings adult a "cup of tea" if asked. Holds and cuddles doll. Kisses doll if adult suggests it. X Replies to adults on phone. X Speaks into phone held by adult. X	✓✓✓✓✓ plays very imaginatively

playladders

name: Beth age 3

nursery area: large space

play activity: trolley

our play for the trolley!

step	repertoire	✓
3	Will play imaginatively with trolley and another child. Will join in an activity with trolley with another child. Will Away leave trolley for another activity.	✓
2	Will allow another child to borrow trolley when busy (adult help) Will "park" trolley to do a short activity Will carry toys in her trolley	✓ ✓ ✓
1	Will help tidy up with trolley Will stop pushing trolley to habit other children X Will allow adult to put something in trolley + Pushes new trolley +	✓

playladders

name:

nursery area:

play activity:

step	repertoire	✓
3		
2		
1		

playladders

name:

nursery area: "LET'S PRETEND" AREA

play activity: Dressing Up

step	repertoire	✓
3	Combines with other activities e.g. spaceman on climbing frame adopted as rocket. Selects clothes to suit an imaginary idea. ("These'll do for .....") Combines into a game (e.g. playing witches) Makes own props to go with outfit e.g. space helmet.	
2	Manages most clothes without help. Speaks as if a different person. Has own ideas and asks for help to develop them. Combines dressing up with simple props e.g. wand. Selects clothes for an idea provided by adult e.g. witch, giant.	
1	Selects special clothes for special activities e.g. aprons- Asks for help e.g. with apron. Allows self to be dressed up. Tries on hats or shoes. Admires self in mirror	

A Practical Guide to Child Observation and Assessment

Children's social development

I. Individual Attributes: The child	Yes	No
1. Is **usually** in a positive mood		
2. Is not **excessively** dependent on the teacher, Nursery Nurse or other adults		
3. **Usually** comes to the nursery or school willingly		
4. **Usually** copes with rebuffs and reverses adequately		
5. Shows the capacity to empathise		
6. Has positive relationship with one or two peers; shows capacity to really care about them, miss them if absent, etc.		
7. Displays the capacity for humour		
8. Does not seem to be acutely or chronically lonely		
II. Social Skill Attributes: The child usually		
1. Approaches the others positively		
2. Expresses wishes and preferences clearly; gives reasons for actions and positions		
3. Asserts own rights and needs appropriately		
4. Is not easily intimidated by bullies		
5. Expresses frustration and anger effectively and without harming others or property		
6. Gains access to ongoing groups at play and work		
7. Enters ongoing discussion on the subject; makes relevant contributions to ongoing activities		
8. Takes turns fairly easily		
9. Shows an interest in others; exchanges information with and requests information from others appropriately		
10. Negotiates and compromises with others appropriately		
11. Does not draw inappropriate attention to self		
12. Accepts and enjoys peers and adults of ethnic groups other than his or her own		
13. Interacts non-verbally with other children with smiles, waves, nods, etc.		
III. Peer Relationship Attributes: The child is		
1. **Usually** accepted versus neglected or rejected by other children		
2. **Sometimes** invited by other children to join them in play, friendship, and work		

D.E. McClellan and L.G. Katz 1992

Sheffield LEA

An Admission Profile

Completion of the profile

It is envisaged that the format can be adapted to meet the specific needs of individual teachers and schools.

The profile is intended to give a general picture of the child and will highlight areas of concern for further work. Teachers will find that the profile does not take very long to complete, particularly as staff become more confident with the range of behaviours illustrated.

From the range of behaviours 1–5 under each sub-heading, choose the number which most clearly represents the stage at which the child is operating. This number should be written on the profile summary grid which follows the section. This profile summary can be completed during the first six weeks after entry and will give a broad overall picture of the child which can be discussed with colleagues, parents and support staff. This profile precedes the developmental record for children in nursery schools and classes.

It is suggested that the profile be completed at the end of the child's settling-in period in school when the staff are aware of the child's behaviour and development in a wide range of activities. A return to this profile at regular intervals would enable staff to monitor the child's progress.

Name . . . .

Date of birth

Admission date

Attendance

Anything particular relating to all-round development

Physical development

Gross motor skills

Description	Rating
Excellent coordination and control, e.g. running, climbing, balancing, throwing, kicking	1
Usually well coordinated	2
Satisfactory	3
Below average, tends to be awkward	4
Very poorly coordinated, clumsy, often falls over, bumps into things	5

Fine motor skills

Description	Rating
Excellent manipulation of pencils, small construction materials	1
Above average control and co-ordination	2
Satisfactory	3
Awkward in fine control and manipulation	4
Very poor fine coordination and manipulative skills, great difficulties in holding small tools	5

Social and emotional development

Cooperation

Description	Rating
Very keen to work/play with others	1
Enjoys working/playing with others	2
Satisfactory	3
Prefers to work/play on own most of time	4
Never (or rarely) works/plays with others	5

Temperament

Description	Rating
Even tempered, nearly always happy and in control of self. Can adapt to new situations, shows initiative, independence	1
Generally happy and controlled, adapts easily and with self confidence	2
Satisfactory	3
Can be irritable and moody in new situations	4
Finds new situations very disturbing, becomes excitable, withdrawn or loses control	5

Acceptance by peers

Description	Rating
Very popular	1
Well accepted member of the group	2
Satisfactory	3
On fringe of peer groups; peers tend to shun him/her	4
Disliked and rejected by peers	5

Attitudes to peers

Description	Rating
Very considerate and thoughtful to others	1
Usually kind and considerate	2
Satisfactory	3
Often wary: can be aggressive in response to others. Tends to avoid other children	4
Always or nearly always disregards others' feelings	5

Attitudes to adults

Description	Rating
Nearly always keen to please, to do well	1
Helpful and cooperative most of the time	2
Satisfactory	3
Can be uncooperative and unresponsive; disruptive on occasions	4
Often refuses to cooperate, can be very disruptive	5

General development and attitude to learning

Degree of involvement in task

1	Excellent attention to task, works well and is not affected by general classroom activity
2	Above average attention to task, only occasionally distracted
3	Satisfactory
4	Below average, tends to look around, gets distracted
5	Very poor ability to attend to one task, highly distracted by noise or movement

Concentration and ability to organise

1	Nearly always concentrates until concluded. Very good ability to organise self
2	Generally concentrates well
3	Satisfactory
4	Attention span limited: problems with organising
5	Very short attention span, tasks usually unfinished, very disorganised

Motivation

1	Very keen to learn, always or nearly always interested in learning tasks
2	Above average eagerness to learn
3	Satisfactory
4	Below average, tends to want to avoid learning situations
5	Apathetic and uninterested, difficult to motivate

Level of concern felt

1	Excellent general development, causes no concern
2	General development is very good
3	Satisfactory
4	Some concern about general development, overall below average
5	General concern about development, overall development is slow

Summary of profile

Score		1	2	3	4	5
Physical development	Gross motor skills					
	Fine motor skills					
Social and emotional development	Cooperation					
	Attitudes to peers					
	Acceptance by peers					
	Temperament					
	Attitudes to adults					
General development and attitudes to learning	Motivation					
	Concentration and ability to organise					
	Degree of involvement in task					
	Level of concern felt					

Any action needed

A Practical Guide to Child Observation and Assessment

Graphs, pie and bar charts and histograms

These can be a useful way of collating information which you might find interesting about a group of children. For example, how do the children travel to school? How many of the children can skip? What is the most used piece of inside or outside equipment? Does the age of the child relate to skill with a pair of scissors?

Sometimes these graphs and charts can be used in reports to managers and parents, giving information about the establishment in an easy-to-digest format. Parents can use pie charts at home, filling in a child's ability to acquire certain skills in order to share the information with the establishment. Charts showing the use the children are making of the equipment provided might help staff to encourage children to use other types of equipment, perhaps putting out more stimulating material.

Advantages
- Quick and easy to collate.
- Easy to read.

Disadvantages
- Most charts only provide information about groups of children.
- They do not give much information about individuals.

Co-operative play

Date: 28.3.01

Method: Histogram

Start time: 9.30 am   Finish time: 3.25 pm

Number of children present: 25

Number of adults present: 2

Permission sought from: Supervisor

Type of setting:

Infant school in an inner-city area with mainly middle class children.

Immediate environment:

In corridor – small library area

First name(s)/initial(s) of child(ren) observed: see list

Brief description of child(ren) observed:

Ages: 6:1 to 6:9

Gender: M and F

Aim of observation:

To observe the reading ability of a group of children.

Example of a histogram.

Name	01	02	03	04	05	06	07	08
Victoria	✓	✓		✓				
Jamilla			✓		✓	✓	✓	
Adem					✓	✓	✓	✓
Joseph			✓		✓			
Colin					✓			
Emma					✓			✓
Nicky			✓		✓		✓	
Mona								✓

Tick list to show individual reading ability on the day

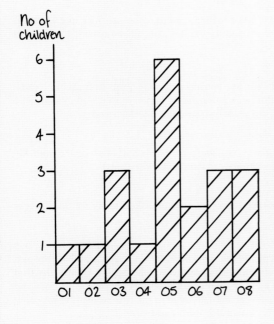

No of children

Key
01 Read in true sense
02 Recognise all 3 letter words
03 Recognise some 3 letter words
04 Recognise all 2 letter words
05 Recognise some 2 letter words
06 Read book from memory
07 Used pictures as prompts
08 Showed no interest

Example of a histogram (continued).

Individual reports in brief

Time: 09.50 Name: Jamilla

Jamilla picked out four books from the basket. The first book, *Round and Round*, was read through quickly. But this was done through memory rather than reading in the true sense. The second book, *Doctors and Nurses*, was more of a challenge. The story was not a familiar one to Jamilla. Some two- and three-letter words were recognised, but Jamilla found it very hard going.

Jamilla used some of the pictures that accompanied the text to work out what was written, and tried very hard.

With the third book, *The Storm*, she was back on familiar ground and read it from memory. Jamilla made a very brave attempt at the last book, *The Pumpkin*, using pictures and recognised words to work out the story. Most of the story line was missed, but Jamilla still did well.

Time: 10.00 Name: Adem

Goldilocks and the Three Bears was Adem's choice from the book basket. This version is a very hard book to read for this age band. Adem picked out this book and started to tell the story from memory of a different version of the story. When stopped, Adem tried to read the book, but was only able to recognise some two- and three-letter words. Adem never really showed any interest in reading today and spent his time looking around.

Time: 10.05 Name: Joseph

Joseph also chose *Goldilocks* as his book. He started enthusiastically enough, but lost interest when he realised that the book was too hard for him. Again, Joseph realised some two- and three-letter words. When offered a second choice of book, Joseph declined and his concentration drifted further away.

Time: 10.15 Name: Colin

Colin was only interested for a very short while. He managed to recognise very few words in the two-letter bracket. After two pages, he started to wander around the corridor, so he was taken back to class.

Time: 10.18 Name: Emma

Emma chose two books, *The Pumpkin* and *Plop*. She started with *Plop*. Emma sat on her hands, legs swinging back and forth. Her attention was never really focused on the books and she showed no real interest. However, Emma did recognise some two-letter words.

Time: 15.10 Name: Nicky

Nicky struggled with the books that he chose. These were *The Storm* and *Round and Round*. He was able to recognise some two- and three-letter words and tried very hard.

Time: 15.15 Name: Mona

Mona didn't want to read at all and appeared too upset when asked to do so. So this was abandoned.

Time: 15.16 Name: Victoria

Victoria picked two books, *The Cat, the Bird and the Tree* and *Animals*. Victoria sailed through these books with ease, pointing to each individual word as she spoke them. On first impressions, I thought that this was done by pure memory. But when checked by asking what other words were, it was evident that Victoria can actually read in the true sense. She was only stopped by a few words, for example 'redbreast' (as for robin) and 'afraid'.

Victoria enjoys reading and was upset when asked to stop as home time loomed closer.

Example of a histogram (continued).

Observation

Histogram

Interpretation

This observation follows a request from the class teacher to take a group of children for reading practice. The children and the books were selected by the teacher, and I took the children one by one out into the corridor. The results were first recorded on a tick list and a brief written report was made for each child. A histogram was added later.

As can be seen from the histogram and the tick list, there is only one child in this group of 6-year-olds who can read fluently. The reports showed that, although there is some variation in ability, there is only real concern about one child, Colin. Some writers, such as Pluckrose (1980), have pointed out that this need not be a cause for concern, as long as the child is attaining well in other areas, for example numeracy and social relationships.

The concentration time span varied but this may be due to the time of day when more interesting activities were going on in the classroom.

Personal learning

I learned how difficult it is to assess in one session children's ability in any learning situation. One has to take into account that the children do not know me very well, we were out in the noisy corridor, interesting activities were happening in the classroom and three of the children appear very tired at this time of day. This has demonstrated to me the strong distractions that hamper a child's concentration, as highlighted in the College handout (1992).

Recommendations

With the teacher's permission, I would like to do a follow-up activity with the same children in a month's time, at a different time of day. I have realised how much opportunity for reading most children need, and that reading is taught and not caught! I will spend some time each day with Colin to build a relationship and, hopefully, he will then be able to relax more with me.

Bibliography

Pluckrose H., 1980, *Children in their Primary Schools*, Harper & Row.
College handout, 1992, 'Becoming a reader'.

Supervisor's signature

P. Wilkinson

Example of a histogram (continued).

Social and emotional development

Date: 10.12.03

Method: Bar chart and narrative

Start time: 1:15   Finish time: 3:15

Number of children present: 10

Number and role of adults present:

   1 teacher, 1 teaching assistant, 1 student

Permission sought from: Supervisor

Type of setting: Infant school

Immediate environment:

   A year 1 classroom

First name(s)/initial(s) of child(ren) observed: B1–5, G1–5

Brief description of child(ren) observed:

Ages: from 5:4 to 6:2

Gender: 5 male, 5 female

Aim of observation:

   To observe children's behaviour in order to create a picture

   of gender preference

Example of an observation using a bar chart.

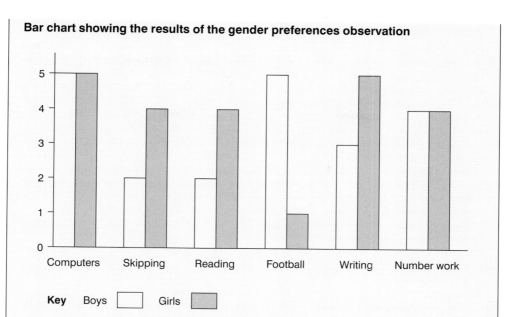

Bar chart showing the results of the gender preferences observation

Key Boys ☐   Girls ▨

Observation

The group is sitting at the table; their chairs are turned to face the teacher. The equipment for the activity they are about to do is placed in the middle of the table, except for the backing card, which G1 has picked up and is holding in her hands. The teacher is giving out the instructions for the activity, which is to make an 'Angel calendar'; these will then be taken home, so that the children can give them as a gift for Christmas. When she has finished, the children on the table (consisting of four boys – B1, B2, B3, B4 – and one girl – G1) turn to look at the material placed in the centre of the table.

G1 starts to give out the coloured card to the other children; the boys are requesting particular colours, and G1 selects a colour for them (I am not sure if it is the colour they requested). She appears to be talking to everyone on the table, although the boys are not replying. Once everyone has been given some card, G1 sits down to start the activity. B1, B2, B3, B4 talk to each other; they are laughing about the colour card they have got. B2 and B3 swap cards; they continue talking.

A teaching assistant (TA) joins the table; all the children stop talking while the TA checks that they know what they are doing. She gets them started on the activity.

TA is helping B1. B2 and B3 are talking; they are comparing their calendars and discussing how they are going to make them and what colours they are going to use.

B3 asks B1 for the glue. B1 passes the glue but doesn't say anything. Then when asked by B3, B1 passes the glitter he has just finished using. The two boys then start to discuss and compare the calendars; they are telling each other what they are going to do next, and who they are going to give them to as a present. G1, who has been talking to TA, then asks B3 for the glue and B4 asks B3 for the glitter. B1 asks TA what he should do next.

B2 and B3 start a conversation. B1 (when he finishes talking to TA) joins in. B4 and TA leave the table (separately). G1 joins in the conversation; they are now talking about the school play, which will be performed later this evening. They are telling each other what their part is and who will be coming to watch them. All the children are still working at their calendars. They are passing around the glitter and glue whilst they are talking. TA returns to the table, G1 stops talking and B1 talks to TA. B4 rejoins the table.

Example of an observation using a bar chart (continued).

Interpretation

From my questioning as shown on the bar chart I was able to see that within the Year 1 class there was no gender stereotyping for the computer or number work, although the girls said they enjoyed number work 'because it is easy', whilst the boys like it 'because it is fun'. This difference in gender abilities is backed up by Papalia and Wendkos Olds (1992, p. 338): 'Girls excel in computation (adding, subtracting, and so on)'.

Some of the boys said that skipping is 'girly and boring', and out of the girls, only one did not enjoy skipping, as it is 'too tiring'. Lindon (2002) observes: 'Girls play games with rules, such as skipping games and there is a competitive feel . . . rather than the direct game-centred competition of football.'

In the group that I questioned, I found that all the boys enjoyed football, and they all followed a particular team. Only one of the girls likes football. She doesn't follow a particular team. This is normal development for children and is backed up by Lindon (2002): 'It is the boys who usually play football . . . although the girls do get involved sometimes.'

I found that the girls preferred reading to the boys. This is backed up by a study from Okehampton College. They found that 'behaviour was related to literacy' and that 'generally boys read little and enjoyed it less, whereas girls derived greater enjoyment from reading and read more' (Kirby, 2000).

Reading can be linked to verbal tasks, such as instructions for writing activities. The girls questioned derived a greater enjoyment from writing than the boys.

In the beginning of my observation of the creative activity I noticed that G1 took control, by distributing the card. This goes against the norm for gender stereotyping, which is often found in children. It is often the boys that take control. This is backed up by Meadows (1986, p. 195): 'only men are forceful and assertive.'

During the observation I found that G1 interacted very little with the boys on the table. As Lindon (2002) says: 'Children in primary school tend to play with their own sex.' However, some of the boys liked to talk with one another: 'Boys talk together . . . they talk about shared interests' (Lindon, 2002).

Throughout the observation, B1 often referred to TA for assistance, guidance and approval. This is the developmental norm for both boys and girls of this age: 'By the age of 5 children usually want the approval of adults' (Beaver et al., 2001, p. 222). Also during the observation, G1 often asked for assistance and spoke with TA: 'On the whole, girls gravitate towards adults more' (Meadows, 1986, p. 197).

Evaluation

In my observation I found that the gender stereotyping, whilst not constant throughout play and activities, is very dominant in social groups and 'who the children talk to' during their lessons. The interaction from TA involved G1 more than would have been the case had the children been alone. The theorist Maccoby backs this up: 'Children use gender as a basis for social grouping without any pressure from adults to do so. Indeed cross-gender interactions occur only when adults explicitly structure the situation to encourage them' (Smith et al., 1998, p. 147). 'Children are trying to make sense of their world and having gained gender identity, they go on to develop a set of rules to understand what this means' (*Nursery World*, 2002).

This observation would have been better in a 'free movement' session or 'free play', where the children could interact with whom they wished, thus giving me a better view of cross-gender interactions.

Personal learning

From this observation, I have learnt that the children I observed are at the stage of development that is normal for their age. I found that most of the children I questioned reacted in similar ways for the boys/girls in the different activities. The children have seen and believe in 'the idea that boys and girls are expected to behave differently' (O'Hagan, 1997, p. 153). I learnt that many of the boys don't like 'girly' activities and many of the girls don't like

Example of an observation using a bar chart (continued).

'boys' games'. I learnt that it is the role of the adult to discourage steriotyping activities and toys. As a childcare worker, I have learnt to encourage children to 'choose toys for interest, not because they are "boys' toys" or "girls' toys".' (O'Hagan, 1997, p. 153). In 1983, Best said: 'Boys must not show any weakness or sentiment, must not cry, must not associate with girls or sissies (boys who associate with girls), must not do feminine activities' (Meadows, 1986, p. 197). As O'Hagan (1997, p. 153) says, 'It is the influence of adults around them that will lead children to view certain toys as unacceptable.'

I found my observation very effective, especially the 'questioning' part. To develop this, next time I would ask the children in a group what activities they like and dislike, seeing how much effect peer pressure has on them at this age.

Next time I do an observation like this, I will question a group of children of mixed race and ages, as well as ability and gender; this will help to avoid any discrimination, and limit the possibility of the children feeling left out. I would also try and observe an activity that is seen as 'boyish' to see if the children react and group differently.

To promote the children's development I would encourage them to follow a good role model and where possible promote interactions with the opposite sex – i.e. by putting them in mixed groups.

Recommendations

To change such stereotypical ideas, views on what boys and girls should say and do must be avoided. Providing books, videos, toys and posters, etc., which show men doing typically female jobs/activities, and show women doing typically male jobs/activities, would provide a good role model for children. 'As well as learning about gender, children also find out what it means to be a boy or girl. Our sex-role concept dictates our actions and attitudes' (*Nursery World*, 2002).

Bibliography

Beaver M. et al., 2001, *Babies and Young Children*, Nelson Thornes.
Kirby R., 2000, www.practicalparent.org.
Lindon, J., 2002, *Understanding Children's Play*, Nelson Thornes.
Meadows S., 1986, *Understanding Child Development*, Routledge.
Nursery World, 19/26 December 2002.
O'Hagan M., 1997, *Geraghty's Caring for Children*, Ballière Tindall.
Papalia D. and Wendkos Olds S., 1992, *A Child's World*, McGraw-Hill.
Smith P. et al., 1998, *Understanding Children's Development*, Blackwell.

Supervisor's signature

M. Johnson

Example of an observation using a bar chart (continued).

Target child

The target child observation technique was invented as a tool to study concentration in pre-school children. This observation was developed in the 1970s as part of the Oxford Pre-school Research Project carried out by Kathy Sylva et al., and described in their book *Childwatching at Playgroup and Nursery School* (1980). The purpose of the research was to find out which activities and settings furthered children's concentration, and which were merely 'passing time'.

You need to watch one particular child and see exactly what activity that child does over a set period of time. Any language used or social interaction is also noted. These two variables may or may not aid the child in concentrating on a particular task for a longer period. See page 91 for a sheet that you may use for the observation.

This technique is a good example of a pre-coded way of collecting data. The Oxford group decided to use certain letters and symbols to denote:

- the child's task, be it art, or story-listening, or watching others with whom she was doing the task (known as the activity record)
- what she was saying and what was said to her (known as the language record)
- what materials she used
- what 'programme' was in force at the time of observation, for example whether it was free play or group story
- whether there were signs of commitment or challenge, such as pursed lips or intent gaze.

The Oxford group listed 30 different activity codes, such as gross motor play, art, and small-scale construction. These codes were devised specifically for the research and would be too complex and time consuming for general use in the establishment. Nevertheless, you might find it an interesting way of closely observing one child, for example a child who used little language, or who did not appear to relate well to children or to adults. Any abbreviations you might use must be noted on your observation.

Advantages

- Gives a more focused example of a child's behaviour.
- Allows observer to focus clearly on one child over a period of time.
- Freedom to add anything that seemed important to the child.
- Shows areas most used by the child in the classroom.
- Shows which setting promotes conversation.
- Simple grid aids analysis.

Disadvantages

- Codes have to be learned and need to be practised before use.
- Observer needs time to focus exclusively on the child.
- Need to develop ability to summarise precisely.

Target child observation

Child's initials:　　　　Sex:　　　　Age:　　　　Date and time observed:

Activity record	Language record	Task	Social
1 min			
2 min			
3 min			
4 min			
5 min			
6 min			
7 min			
8 min			

You may photocopy this sheet for your own use. © Nelson Thornes Ltd.

How a child spends his day

Date: 13.11.03

Method:

Target child. I shall observe the child for ten minutes every hour, for a total of six hours. This method will enable me to focus on one particular child, following exactly what activities/experiences he will partake in throughout the day.

Start time: 10:00   Finish time: 4:00

Number of children present: 1 (11)

Number and role of adults present:

The four childcare practitioners, 'baby room' manager and myself were present.

Permission sought from: Supervisor

Type of setting:

The nursery is privately run. It is situated near a busy high street, yet the surrounding area is relatively quiet, with semi-detached houses on the opposite street. There is also a zebra crossing close to the nursery, ensuring safety for those who use it.

Immediate environment:

It is 10:00 am, and the babies are engaged in various experiences. Some are playing with the toy telephones on the carpet, while others are being held by staff members or sleeping in their cots.

Example of a target child observation.

First name(s)/initial(s) of child(ren) observed: P

Brief description of child(ren) observed:

Ages: 11 months

Gender: Male

Brief description of baby observed:

- P joined the nursery in May 2003.
- Both his parents are British.
- He has one older sister, who also attends the nursery.
- He is generally in good health.
- He is a very lively and friendly baby, who enjoys the company of adults and the babies present in the nursery. He always participates fully in the activities/experiences that have been set up in the 'baby room'. He is also a confident walker, and uses some language.

Aim of observation:

To observe how P spends his day at nursery, for example the activities he undertakes, how much time he spends interacting with staff, sleeping, having his nappy changed and feeding.

I want to carry out this observation in order to see how much time is spent in the above areas, which will in turn enable me to draw my conclusions and recommend further activities to enhance particular aspects of the child's development, as well as discussing matters that may arise from my observation, for example, if there is little interaction with the baby and the adults in the setting.

Example of a target child observation (continued).

Target child observation

Child's initials: P   Sex: M   Age: 0:11   Date and time observed: 13.11.03

10 minutes each hour for six hours

Hour 1

Time	Activity/experience	Physical	Intellectual	Language	Emotional	Social
1 min	PS in garden centre	Grabs carrot and slots it through letterbox	Sol	Sil but Sm	Appears content Sm	WO
2 min	FS (milk)	Grasps bottle with left hand	Looking down at his bottle	Ba "Beeeah"	WO	S Sol
3 min	Still FS S (on carpet)	Securely holds bottle with left hand	WO	Sm waving arms up and down	Sm at me then turns to Jem	Points at toy Jem is playing with
4 min	FS	Picks up toy phone, puts it to his ear	Understands its use	Ba "Dabdaboo!"	WO while Ba	Sol
5 min	FS	S on edge of ball pond	Keeps an eye on his bottle!	Sil, looks at bottle while drkinking	Appears content	Sol
6 min	W	PS at safety gate	Knows not to pass through it!	Ba "Aahh!"	Sm at me	Sol
7 min	Plays with large red spongy car	Cw rapidly to centre of carpet	Manipulating, squeezes the car	Ba "Dahdah"	Sm at car	Sol
8 min	Now plays with large yellow truck	"Swings" truck from right to left	Rolls truck wheels with his hands	Shakes head; "Nah!"	Sm	Par sits close by to Emma
9 min	S In ball pond, in front of mirror	Throws large ball out of "pond"	Recognises himself in mirror Sm	Ba "Ha ha!"	Sm	Sol
10 min	S In ball pond, in front of mirror	Is balancing on "edge" of pond wall	WO	Ba	Happy, Sm	Sol

Ba – Babbling   FF – Finger Food   NC – Nappy changing   Sl – Sleeping
BC – Being carried   FS – Feeding self   Par – Parallel play   Sm – Smiling
BH – Being held   IA – Interaction with adult   PS – Pulls to stand   Sol – Solitary play
Cr – Crying   IP – Interaction with peers   S – Sitting   W – Walking
Cw – Crawling   MO – Mouthing objects   Sil – Silent   WO – Watching others

A Practical Guide to Child Observation and Assessment

Target child observation (continued)

Hour 2

Time	Activity/experience	Physical	Intellectual	Language	Emotional	Social
1 min	Carpet play	MO	Exploring the play materials	Ba	Sm	Par
2 min	Carpet play	MO	A means of exploring the play materials	Ba	Sm	Par
3 min	Garden centre	Grabs at "potted flowers"	Appears frustrated now	Ba	Appears quite angry	IP
4 min	Garden centre	Baby snatches these from P	"Pushes" the baby to get out	Ba	Appears quite angry	IP
5 min	S (Near Duplo blocks on carpet)	Rolls Duplo car across carpet	WO	Sil	Focuses on the car	Sol
6 min	S (Still amongst Duplo play)	Bangs two blocks together	WO	Sil	Laughs out loud	Sol
7 min	FF FS	Hits his hands on tray and kicks his legs out	Bangs on table – sees food arriving!	Ba	Sm	IA
8 min	FF FS	Eats nuggett by grasping and squashing it	Looks at nuggetts while eating	Ba	Looks content	IA
9 min	FF FS	Eats with right hand, left "smashes" the tray	Wonder, converses with P "Is that nice?!"	Ba	Chuckles at her voice intonations	IA
10 min	FF FS	Is given waffles, discarding nuggetts	Eats while WO	Ba	Sm	IA

Ba – Babbling	FF – Finger Food	NC – Nappy changing	Sl – Sleeping
BC – Being carried	FS – Feeding self	Par – Parallel play	Sm – Smiling
BH – Being held	IA – Interaction with adult	PS – Pulls to stand	Sol – Solitary play
Cr – Crying	IP – Interaction with peers	S – Sitting	W – Walking
Cw – Crawling	MO – Mouthing objects	Sil – Silent	WO – Watching others

Hour 3

Time	Activity/experience	Physical	Intellectual	Language	Emotional	Social
1 min	Cw over to slide	Stands (leaning on side)	Looks at slide	Sil (Sm)		Sol
2 min	Slide	Manages to crawl right through	Looks pleased, claps!	Ba to me	Laughs out loudly	I encourage P to Cw through it
3 min	S on carpet and plays with phone	Dials numbers	Ba into the phone	Ba "Hiya!"	Looks at baby (WO)	Par
4 min	Plays with phone		Looks at me while talking into phone	Ba "Yeahyeah!"		Sol
5 min	IA (while standing at safety gate)	Stands while grasping bars on gate	Engages in a "conversation"	Ba	Sm	Holds adult's hand
6 min	IA	BH	Appears very content	Ba	Chuckling, looks very happy	Close bond with adult
7 min	Carpet area BH	Sits on adult's lap	Watches her	Ba	Seems content	Sol
8 min	W into dining area	Walks a few steps, topples then carries on	Knows he shouldn't be in here!	Sil but Sm	Chuckles, continues to Ba	Sol
9 min	Plays with large blue ball	Rolls and throws the ball		Ba		Sol
10 min	Continues to play with ball	Cw after it!	Chases ball yet rolls it further away	Ba	Appears content	Sol

Ba – Babbling	FF – Finger Food	NC – Nappy changing	Sl – Sleeping
BC – Being carried	FS – Feeding self	Par – Parallel play	Sm – Smiling
BH – Being held	IA – Interaction with adult	PS – Pulls to stand	Sol – Solitary play
Cr – Crying	IP – Interaction with peers	S – Sitting	W – Walking
Cw – Crawling	MO – Mouthing objects	Sil – Silent	WO – Watching others

Target child observation (continued)

Hour 4

Time	Activity/experience	Physical	Intellectual	Language	Emotional	Social
1 min	S on carpet	Stacks one brick onto another	Looks at bricks "Haaa"	Ba	Happy, Sm	Sol
2 min	S on carpet	Cw across carpet	Sees key worker	Sil	Hugs adult's leg!	Watches her play with stacking toy
3 min	Cw now	Reaches for Teletubby figure	Pulls head off, MO	Sil	Looks content, Sm	Par – plays beside two babies
4 min	P falls over BH	Worker trips over stacking toy	P is upset as he has tripped, Cr	P is silent	Cr	Adult comforts him
5 min	S in ball pond	Throws balls out, one by one	Runs towards his milk, has understood the adult	Ba	Chuckles	Sol
6 min	(S) FS carpet	Holds bottle with left hand, right hand strokes carpet	WO	Sil	Sm, looks very happy!	Sol
7 min	(S) FS carpet	Still strokes carpet in large movements	WO	Sil (very involved in drinking)	Appears content again	Sol
8 min	(S) FS carpet	Throws his bottle on carpet	Seems to have had enough!	Ba "Aaah!"	WO	WO
9 min	Cw back to ball pond	Throws balls out	Throws ball to me, I roll it back	Sm, Ba	Excitedly throws out balls	IA
10 min	S in ball pond	Grasps and throws the largest ball out	Having managed this he claps for himself	Sil	Looks very happy	Par (is close to other babies)

Ba – Babbling	FF – Finger Food	NC – Nappy changing	Sl – Sleeping
BC – Being carried	FS – Feeding self	Par – Parallel play	Sm – Smiling
BH – Being held	IA – Interaction with adult	PS – Pulls to stand	Sol – Solitary play
Cr – Crying	IP – Interaction with peers	S – Sitting	W – Walking
Cw – Crawling	MO – Mouthing objects	Sil – Silent	WO – Watching others

Target child observation (continued)

Hour 5

Time	Activity/experience	Physical	Intellectual	Language	Emotional	Social
1 min	FF FS	Uses pincer grip to pick up his peas!	When P drops his food he picks it back up	Ba	Looks happy!	IP
2 min	FF FS	Uses both hands equally to eat his food	Shows he dislikes celery – spits it out!	Ba	Reaches out hand to baby sitting next to him	IP
3 min	FF FS	Holds spoon but does not manage to feed himself	Clearly understands the purpose of a spoon	Ba	Sm, kicks feet out	IP
4 min	SI	SI	SI	SI	SI	SI
5 min	SI	SI	SI	SI	SI	SI
6 min	SI	SI	SI	SI	SI	SI
7 min	NC	Rapidly moves his arms up and down	Adult and P engage in "conversation"	Ba	Very happy, excited	IA
8 min	BC	Close contact between them	Clearly comfortable with key worker	Ba	Happy, Sm	IA
9 min	BC	While being held, P hugs worker	P touches adult's face as she speaks to him	Ba	Happy, Sm	IA
10 min	S on carpet	MO	WO	Sil	Seems content	Sol

Ba – Babbling	FF – Finger Food	NC – Nappy changing	SI – Sleeping
BC – Being carried	FS – Feeding self	Par – Parallel play	Sm – Smiling
BH – Being held	IA – Interaction with adult	PS – Pulls to stand	Sol – Solitary play
Cr – Crying	IP – Interaction with peers	S – Sitting	W – Walking
Cw – Crawling	MO – Mouthing objects	Sil – Silent	WO – Watching others

A Practical Guide to Child Observation and Assessment

Hour 6

Time	Activity/experience	Physical	Intellectual	Language	Emotional	Social
1 min	Cw back to carpet. Plays with soft red car	Cw rapidly while pushing it	Looks happy to be chasing the car!	Sil	Appears engrossed in the car	Par
2 min	NC	Kicks out his legs	MO (brush)	Cr	IA (Adult comforts P)	IA
3 min	NC	Waves his arms up and down	Seems distressed	Cr	IA (Adult comforts P)	IA
4 min	Rapidly Cw back to carpet to play with car again!	Cw faster than when he W	Seems to have remembered this car	Sil	Sm as he begins to play with it	Sol
5 min	BH	Closeness of P and adult	P looks happy as he holds on to Worker	Ba back to adult	Has calmed down, Sm	IA
6 min	Cw back to carpet . . . plays with red car again!	Combines Cw with W (very fast)	Clearly immense enjoyment from this car	Ba	Cuddles the spongy car	Sol
7 min	W	W confidently	W over to his key worker	Ba "Dede!"	Sm	IA
8 min	W	"Dodges" toys scattered on the carpet	Laughs at adult's jokes!	Ba	Sm	IA
9 min	MO while W on carpet	Grasps large tin with both hands	Concentrates on grasping tin	Sil	WO	Sol
10 min	MO while W on carpet	Transfers it to left hand and takes another	Watches tin closely as he swaps hands	Sil	WO	Sol

Ba – Babbling	FF – Finger Food	NC – Nappy changing	Sl – Sleeping
BC – Being carried	FS – Feeding self	Par – Parallel play	Sm – Smiling
BH – Being held	IA – Interaction with adult	PS – Pulls to stand	Sol – Solitary play
Cr – Crying	IP – Interaction with peers	S – Sitting	W – Walking
Cw – Crawling	MO – Mouthing objects	Sil – Silent	WO – Watching others

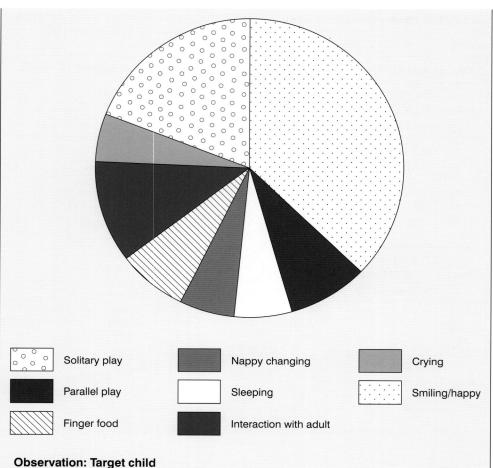

○○ ○	Solitary play		Nappy changing		Crying
	Parallel play		Sleeping	⋅⋅⋅	Smiling/happy
⫽⫽	Finger food		Interaction with adult		

Observation: Target child
Interpretation

Having completed this observation, I have found that P is at his normative age/stage of development. For example, he spent a great deal of the day engaged in babbling, be it with an adult, or to himself. As Minnet (1985, p. 138) observes, 'at eleven months, babies get pleasure out of using their voices and often spend hours making noises (babbling) to themselves. They also make noises to attract attention, and they enjoy holding "conversations" with anyone whose attention they can capture.'

P also showed an understanding of humour within various interactions with his key worker, laughing at her as she spoke in various tones and tickled him. As stated by Lindon (1993, p. 45), 'during the second six months of life, children will flourish with close and affectionate contact with adults who model positive behaviour in communication – they need adults who will give opportunities for a genuine two-way exchange and let the child lead the exchange sometimes'.

There was, however, one surprising event in P's day, this being that he slept a lot less than usual, which in turn caused him to be quite restless at times. He also spent a majority of his day engaged in solitary play, be it with the toys that were laid out on the carpet, or playing in the ball pond by himself. As Tassoni and Beith (1999, p. 258) state, 'between the ages of 0–2 years, children play alone with the reassurance of an adult being close by. They explore the world around them and enjoy adult directed games such as peek-a-boo.'

Example of a target child observation (continued).

There was much time spent interacting with the adult – which was reassuring to see, as the nursery is often very busy with up to 12 babies present on some days. It was clear that P's key worker gained as much pleasure from their interactions as he did. As noted by Catron and Allen (1993, p. 176), 'An open and flexible environment that includes an emphasis on nurturing adult–child relationships enables a young child to reach out in trust to others as well as to respond to appropriate expressions of care from adults'.

The pie chart also shows that roughly the same amount of time was spent on all routine activities, such as feeding, nappy changing and sleeping, and that P spent only a few minutes crying during the day but three times as much was spent in a happy, smiley mood! I believe that this generally 'happy mood' is due to the fact that the staff work in close *partnership* with all *parents* in the setting. One way in which this is achieved is through the staff liaising with parents at the end of each day; this is done partly with the help of the baby's chart (this has information on feeding, mood, sleep times, etc.). The nursery has an open-door policy, making it as easy as possible for parents to come in and discuss matters concerning the welfare of their child. If, for example, the baby experienced some upset during the day, this too would be discussed, in order for parents and staff to deal with the cause of the upset. The setting also holds a parents' evening every three months, which again provides a forum to discuss any matters of concern, and to monitor the child's general progress.

As Neaum and Tallack (1997, p. 49) observe:

Staff and parents need to exchange information about individual children on a regular basis. Events in a child's life such as a new baby, illness in the family or a parent working away from home may all affect behaviour in the pre-school setting. If staff are aware of this they are better able to respond to the child's needs. Other benefits of working with parents include:

- Parents have the most knowledge and understanding of their children; sharing this knowledge with staff enables them to build on previous experience in planning for the child's future development.
- Children are more likely to feel settled and secure if it is clear that there are good channels of communication between parents and staff.

It is therefore clear that this partnership must be implemented effectively by *all* staff, with *all* parents, if there is to be *equality of opportunity* for the children in the setting, as it was in P's case. No matter how hectic the day became, his key worker always made the time and effort to tend to his *physical, intellectual, language, emotional* and *social* care needs. Malik (1998, p. 55) says:

Good practice means promoting equal opportunities and this is achieved by implementing anti-discriminatory practices. It means putting equal opportunities into action, which requires knowledge and understanding of the principles and practices necessary to achieve the objectives.

This involves:

- A knowledge of equal rights legislation, your responsibilities under that legislation and putting them into practice.
- Using language and resources in the early years setting which promote equal opportunities.
- Taking part in regular staff development, appraisal and review sessions to maintain standards of good practice.

Meeting of stated aim

Looking back at my aim, I see that I have achieved all that I set out to do. That is, to observe P during his typical day at nursery – with regard to his time spent interacting with adults, sleeping, playing and eating. I then summarised this information in pie chart form.

Example of a target child observation (continued).

Evaluation of selected method

Having completed this observation, I must say that it was *the most inappropriate* method to use. There was much information that I wanted to include which this method did not allow for, as my list of codes would have been far too lengthy. I also found it quite tricky to concentrate on observing P and remember the codes at the same time. The whole process therefore became quite monotonous.

There are, however, advantages to this method too, as identified by Beaty (1998, p. 51):

- It gives a more focused example of a child's behaviour.
- Allows observer to focus clearly on one child.
- Shows areas most used by child.
- Shows which setting promotes conversation.

Alternative methods that I could have used include the time sample; this would have enabled me to analyse the interpreted data far quicker, rather than comparing the list of codes with the observation itself and the pie chart in order to see the 'whole picture'. Other advantages, as identified by Hobart and Frankel (1999, p. 63), include:

- A collection of precise data.
- More closely focused.
- When completed, data is readily accessible.
- Easily understood by other professionals and parents/carers.
- Professional appearance and format.

A checklist also could have been used. This would have enabled me to observe P for longer periods, while obtaining concise data that can be quickly read and understood by those concerned. Beaty (1998, p. 26) lists other advantages of this method:

- A quick way of presenting a great deal of information.
- Results are obvious and readily understandable.
- Can be useful to combine with a longitudinal observation when carrying out a child study.

Although all the above methods have their advantages and disadvantages, they are each of some value to the observer, as they all provide information on the child observed, but in different contexts.

I also feel that I carried out my observation as objectively as possible.

Recommendations

From my interpreted information, I can see no areas of concern within P's day, as he gets plenty of affection, is fed and changed regularly and gets enough stimulation through engaging in various types of play during his day at nursery.

It may be an idea to plan more focused play experiences for small groups of babies, in order to encourage/promote peer interaction, for the future, as P spent most of his time engaging in solitary play (which at this time is developmentally appropriate). As Tassoni and Beith (1999, p. 171) observe:

Adults have a strong role in helping children to relate to each other. Children are more likely to share and make friendships if they are part of a happy environment – this means there should be a commitment to equal opportunities so children can learn to be understanding and accepting of others . . . some activities are particularly good for making children part of a group, or for helping them to cooperate – for example sand/water play.

Also, it may be beneficial to the baby if there was an outing during the day, although sometimes the weather will not permit this. The opportunity must be taken when the weather is pleasant enough, as fresh air is vital for children; it will also give them a whole new world to experience/be a part of. Catron and Allen (1993, p. 139) say that 'When planning daily

Example of a target child observation (continued).

routines for children in their care, childcare practitioners should aim to provide for the all round needs of the children. This includes the provision of stimulating activities, outings and various outdoor activities.'

Bibliography

Beaty J., 1998, *Observing the Development of the Young Child*, Prentice Hall.
Catron C. and Allen J., 1993, *Early Childhood Curriculum*, Prentice Hall.
Hobart C. and Frankel J., 1999, *A Practical Guide to Child Observation*, 2nd edition, Stanley Thornes.
Lindon J., 1993, *Nursery World*,
Minett P., 1985, *Child Care and Development*, John Murray.
Tassoni P. and Beith K., 1999, *Nursery Nursing*, Heinemann Childcare.

Supervisor's signature

S. Thomas

Example of a target child observation (continued).

5 Further observation techniques

This chapter covers:

- Longitudinal studies
- Sociograms
- Movement and flow charts
- Media
- The High/Scope technique

Learning outcomes

Sometimes the most common forms of assessment and observation do not provide sufficient detail and are not useful enough in helping you to plan for a child's learning and development. This chapter describes some other techniques you might use.

Longitudinal studies

A longitudinal study takes place over a period of time. It can last a few weeks, or a year or more. The reason for doing these studies is to look at the progress of a child in one or more areas of development: for example, to study the locomotive skills of a baby from birth until two years, or to record a child's all-round development over a period of time, as in a child study. This will help you to have a more holistic approach, as you chart the developing skills of one particular child.

You need to have a clear idea of what you hope to achieve by carrying out this study and to discuss this with your supervisor, assessor or tutor. In general terms, you should choose a 'normal' child from a stable family which is unlikely to move away from the area and one to whom you can gain easy access. It is vital to discuss the project with the parents of the child, to gain not only their permission but also, it is hoped, their cooperation and participation. Many parents appreciate a copy of the finished study.

Advantages

- Getting to know the child and the background really well and being able to understand the influence of the family on the child's acquisition of skills.

- A better understanding of developmental norms and how some areas of development may be in advance of others at certain times.
- Closely recording developmental changes over a period of time.
- A detailed, more closely focused knowledge of one child, and an insight into the uniqueness of the individual.
- If through your observations you uncover an area of concern, you may be able to ensure that help is offered earlier than it might otherwise have been.
- The parents' participation allows them to have a better understanding of the child's needs.

Disadvantages

- The baby or child might move away, or become ill. For these reasons, it is sensible to start initially with two children.
- The parents may find continuous observations rather irksome and relationships may become strained.
- Your objective observations may upset the parents.
- It may be easier to identify this child, thus raising issues of confidentiality.
- If a child's development or behaviour proves to be atypical, this may give you a distorted view of developmental norms and normal behaviour.
- Previous knowledge of the child and family can lead to bias from the observer.

Issues

- Being so closely concerned with the family may cause conflict with your professional role. For example, you may exaggerate the child's achievements in order to please a family who have gone out of their way to be helpful.
- Do not record details that are irrelevant to the study of the child, for example the parents' contraceptive history.
- You need to be aware of the child-rearing patterns of different cultures and religions and the wide range of parenting styles.
- Avoid stereotyping children and their families.

A longitudinal study may consist of a number of written observations, checklists, a target child study, a sample of behaviour, and so on, recording a child's development and learning over a period of time. Pages 106–107 are an example of a structured longitudinal study based on the approach devised by the College of Education at the University of Illinois.

ASSESSING PRESCHOOLERS' DEVELOPMENT

Parents often ask how they can tell if their children's development is proceeding "normally". Preschool teachers and day care workers also ask for guidelines to help assess their pupils' progress. To address this problem, Dr Lilian G. Katz and her coauthors suggest that one way of getting a good picture of whether a child's development is going well is by looking carefully at his or her behaviour along the eleven dimensions outlined below. * One word of caution, however: the <u>authors urge that any judgements about a child's progress should be made not on the basis of one or two days of observation, but rather on a longer period. A good general rule is that one week of observation for each year of the child's life will be sufficient for making an initial assessment</u>. For example, if <u>the child is three years old, observations should be conducted over a period of three weeks: four years old, for four weeks and so forth.</u>

Sleeping

Does the child fall asleep and wake up rested, ready to get on with life? While occasional restlessness, nightmares, or grouchy mornings are normal, an average pattern of deep sleep resulting in morning eagerness is a good sign that the child finds life satisfying.

Eating

Does the child eat with appetite? Skipping meals or refusing food on occasion is normal: sometimes the child is too busy with other activities to welcome mealtime or perhaps is more thirsty than hungry at a given moment. However, a child who over a period of weeks eats compulsively or who constantly fusses about the menu is likely to have "got off on the wrong foot". The purpose of eating should be to fuel the system adequately in order to be able to get on with life; food should not dominate adult/child interaction. Keep in mind that children, like many adults, may eat a lot at one meal and hardly anything at the next. These fluctuations do not warrant comment or concern as long as there is reasonable balance in the nutrition obtained.

Toilet Habits

On the average, over a number of weeks, does the child have bowel and bladder control? The random "accident" is no cause for alarm, especially if there are obvious mitigating circumstances, such as excessive intake of liquids, intestinal upset, or simply absorption in ongoing activities to the point of disregarding such "irrelevancies". Persistent lack of control, on the other hand, may suggest the need for adult intervention.

Range of Affect

Does the child exhibit a range of emotions: joy, anger, sorrow, excitement, and so forth? A child whose emotions are of low intensity or whose affect is "flat" or unfluctuating – always angry always sour, always cheerful and enthusiastic – may be having difficulties. Within a range of emotions, the capacity for sadness, to use one example, indicates the ability to make use of correlate emotions: attachment and caring. Both are important signs of healthy development; the inability to experience them may signal the beginning of depression.

Variations in Play

Does the child's play vary over a period of weeks, with the addition of some new elements even though he or she may play with many of the same toys or materials? Increasing elaboration of the same play activities or engagement in a wide variety of activities indicates sufficient inner security to manipulate (literally, to "play with") the environment. If a child stereotypically engages in the same sequence of play, using the same elements in the same ways, he or she may be emotionally "stuck in neutral" and may be in need of temporary help.

Curiosity

Does the child occasionally exhibit curiosity and even mischief? A child who never pokes at the environment or never snoops into new territory – perhaps in fear of punishment or as a result of the over-development of conscience – may not be developing optimally. Curiosity signals a healthy search for boundaries.

---

* Written while Dr Katz was Fulbright Visiting Professor, the paper "Assessing Preschoolers' Development" is coauthored by staff members of the Department of Child Development, Faculty of Home Science, M.S., University of Baroda, Gujarat, India. The full text of the paper from which this short report has been derived is available in ERIC as ED 226 857.

ERIC/EECE, College of Education, University of Illinois, 805 W. Pennsylvania Ave., Urbana. IL 61801

Acceptance of Authority

Does the child usually accept adult authority? Although the inability to yield to adults may constitute a problem, occasional resistance, assertion of personal desires, or expression of objections indicates healthy socialization. Always accepting adult demands and restrictions without a word may suggest excessive anxiety, fear, or perhaps a weakening of self-confidence.

Friendship

Can the child initiate, maintain, and enjoy a relationship with one or more other children? Playing alone some of the time is fine as long as the child is not doing so because of insufficient competence in relating to others. However, chronic reticence in making friends may create difficulties in the development of social competence or relationship building later on, and is cause for concern.

Interest

Is the child capable of sustained involvement and interest in something outside of himself or herself? Does the child's capacity for interest seem to be increasing to allow longer periods of involvement in activity, games, or play? The emphasis here is on "activities" rather than "passivities", such as television watching. A tendency toward increasing involvement in activities requiring a passive role or the persistent inability to see a project to completion may signal difficulties requiring adult intervention.

Spontaneous Affection

Does the child express spontaneous affection for one or more of those with whom he or she spends time? While demonstrations of affection vary among families and cultures, a child whose development is going well is likely on occasion to let others know that they are loved and to express the feeling that the world is a gratifying place. Excessive expressions of this kind, however, may signal doubts about the strength of attachment between adult and child, and may call for consideration.

Enjoyment of the "Good Things of Life"

Is the child capable of enjoying the potentially "good things of life", such as playing with others, going on picnics, exploring new places, and so forth? A child may have a specific problem – fear of insects or food dislikes, for example – but if the problem does not prevent the child from participating in and enjoying life, then it is reasonable to assume it will be outgrown.

The first three dimensions of development – sleeping, eating, and toilet habits – are particularly sensitive indicators of the child's development, since these the child alone controls. The remaining dimensions, more culture-bound and situationally determined, are still of great value in evaluation, since they are likely to represent important goals held for the child by both parents and teachers.

While the dimensions outlined above provide a useful place to begin in evaluating preschoolers' development, it is important to note that difficulties in any one of these categories, or even in several, are not automatic cause for alarm. Such problems should not be interpreted as signalling an irreversible trend; indeed, temporary difficulties often help those close to the child to understand when the child's situation does not match his or her emerging needs, thus assisting in the process of helping the child "get back on the right foot".

RELATED ERIC DOCUMENTS

Bagbahn, Marcia. *Language Development and Early Encounters with Written Language*. (ED 211 975, 24p).

Blevins, Belinda, and Cooper, Robert G., Jr. *The Development of the Ability to Make Transitive Inferences*. (ED 218 919, 11p) 1981.

Burke, Julie, and Clark, Ruth Anne. *Construct System Development, Understanding of Strategic Choices, and the Quality of Persuasive Messages in Childhood and Adolescence*. (ED 210 727, 19p) 1981.

Katz, Phyllis A. *Development of Children's Racial Awareness and Intergroup Attitudes*. (ED 207 675, 55p) 1981.

Proctor, Adele. *Linguistic Input: A Comprehensive Bibliography*. (ED 222 282, 37P) 1982.

Wagner, Betty S. *Developmental Assessment of Infants and Toddlers in Child Care Programs*. (ED 223 565, 21p) 1982.

Date: 10.1.01 to 4.2.01

Method: Child study. Pre-schooler's assessment

Start time: Week 1   Finish time: Week 4

Number of children present: 20 in nursery class

Number of adults present: 2 (+ student) in nursery class

Permission sought from: Supervisor and parent

Type of setting:

Nursery class in inner city school

Immediate environment:

N/A

First name(s)/initial(s) of child(ren) observed: Martha

Brief description of child(ren) observed:

Ages: 4:3

Gender: F

Aim of observation:

To observe and assess a 4-year-old child at nursery

and through consultation with parents at home.

Example of a child study.

Pre-school assessment

Section: One

Sleeping

Week 1 Nursery	Home
Martha is usually full of energy in the nursery, needing no sleep during the day. It is rare to see Martha in a bad or upset mood; this week was typical of that. She has been happy most of the time, only showing signs of tiredness towards the end of the days.	At home Martha has no fixed bed time; it is variable depending on how tired she is. Sometimes she is very tired and can fall asleep as soon as she comes home from nursery, sometimes she is still awake at 22:00 hrs. Food has the effect of waking her up. Her mother tells me that at times it is a fight to keep her awake to eat but, as soon as she has eaten, she is wide awake again. A late night does not always mean that she is tired the next day/evening.
Week 2	
As above. Only difference is that Martha now comes to the school at 08:00 hrs every day as her mother works in the Early Years Centre in the school.	On Sunday Martha was tired during the day and wanted to sleep. Martha's mother took her to the park and stopped her from sleeping. Martha perked up while in the park. In the evening she was still wide awake at 22:00 hrs; she couldn't sleep.
Week 3	
Martha was unusually tired on the Monday of this week, but was as usual the rest of the week.	Had a couple of late nights this week; other than that no change.
Week 4	
No change.	Nothing unusual.

Example of a child study (continued).

Pre-school assessment

Section: Two

Eating

Week 1 Nursery	Home
Martha has eaten well this week at the nursery. There has been no refusal of any food and the amounts are of standard size. Martha never rushes to the dinner table and finishes eating at about the same time as the other children.	Martha has eaten well at home this week. This is standard for her. She has never been really fussy about anything and her appetite is normally good.
Week 2	
As above.	No change.
Week 3	
No change.	Martha's mother told me that Martha has food fads at times, going on to and off some things. This week she was a little bit fussy about peanut butter. She no longer likes it.
Week 4	
No change.	No change.

Example of a child study (continued).

Pre-school assessment

Section: Three

Toileting

Week 1　　　Nursery	Home
There have been no accidents at all in the nursery this week. Martha always goes to the toilet in good time while in the nursery.	Martha's mother tells me that Martha still has the occasional accident at home and that she wets the bed frequently.
Week 2	
As above.	No accidents this week, but has wet the bed on a couple of occasions.
Week 3	
No change.	No change.
Week 4	
No change.	No change.

Example of a child study (continued).

Pre-school assessment

Section: Four

Range of affect

Week 1 Nursery	Home
Martha is usually a happy child in play and is always ready to socialise with adults. Martha shows concern and sadness if a playfriend is hurt or is crying. This week Martha accidentally ran over a child's ankle with a pram; she said sorry right away and displayed remorse for having hurt the other child.	Martha saw a child psychologist at one stage in her past. This was for uncontrollable rage or severe temper tantrums. By all accounts, these tantrums were brought on from moving house, or so the mother was led to believe by the psychologist. Other than this, at home Martha loves to mother younger children and babies and is normally happy.
Week 2	
Martha threw a tantrum this week in the nursery playground. This was because her mother and I were covering the sand pit and she wanted to help but was unable to. She was screaming and shouting at us. Her mother said that this was only because she (mum) was there and had it been myself and another person, this would not have taken place. This was the only occurrence.	Martha threw a tantrum at home when she wanted mum to join in with her game; mum was otherwise occupied.
Week 3	
Nothing to report.	No change.
Week 4	
Nothing to report.	Martha is more demanding of her mother's time since she has started working in the Early Years Centre, but has still a full range of affections.

Example of a child study (continued).

Pre-school assessment

Section: Five

Variations to play

Week 1 Nursery	Home
Martha just loves toys of any description. She also enjoys playing without toys, for example climbing, running. This week has seen Martha riding a tricycle, pushing a pram, playing on a see-saw and working on the activity tables, both alone and with others.	Loves her toys and is possessive of them. She plays with all of them, not at the same time of course, but she never neglects any of them. Martha talks while playing alone, normally playing the part of the adult, telling the children to do various things. She likes her puzzles and books at home. She also paints and draws.
Week 2	
This week we introduced the use of woodwork tools and wood. Martha was keen to join in, and did. She also got involved with other children who were playing with a tent outside in the garden. This was used as 'a house' in their game. Martha used her imagination by 'going shopping' from the house.	No change at home.
Week 3	
Martha spent a lot of time in the Early Years Centre this week. She likes to play with the younger children.	Spends time playing with all her toys at home. This week is no exception.
Week 4	
No change.	No change.

Example of a child study (continued).

Pre-school assessment

Section: Six

Curiosity

Week 1 Nursery	Home
Martha wants to know about anything and everything. If a child is hurt, Martha is there to ask why and who. Martha is usually one of the first to investigate anything new in the nursery. Nothing outstanding has happened this week.	Martha asks lots of why type questions at home; she is very inquisitive. She asks a lot of questions about her Gran, who died a little while ago. Martha thinks that her Gran now lives underground and that she still has a house there, still goes shopping, etc.
Week 2	
Martha was one of the first to investigate the woodwork table and asked what was being made, what the tools were called and what the vice was for, etc.	No change, nothing outstanding.
Week 3	
No change.	Still as curious as ever.
Week 4	
No change.	No change.

Example of a child study (continued).

Pre-school assessment

Section: Seven

Acceptance of authority

Week 1 Nursery	Home
Usually Martha never argues with the adults in the nursery. She will ask why she has to do things, but always does them.	At home, it really depends on what is being asked of her. She 'will try it on' but knows how much she can get away with and when not to argue.
Week 2	
No change in attitude.	Nothing has changed at home.
Week 3	
No change.	No change.
Week 4	
No change.	No change.

Example of a child study (continued).

Pre-school assessment

Section: Eight

Friendship

Week 1 Nursery	Home
Martha is usually an outgoing, friendly child who gets on with all the children in the nursery. Martha enjoys the company of others, but on occasion plays alone. Now and then Martha plays with the younger children and takes care of them.	Martha is not allowed out at present as the family live in a maisonette and it would be hard to supervise her. She still sees other children and makes friends easily, but not as much as before. She likes to play with children who are younger than herself and tends to try to mother them.
Week 2	
Martha has been playing with children in the Early Years Room more than with her own peer group this week. She spends a lot of time there with her mother, but is not dependent on her.	No change.
Week 3	
Martha has spent equal time in both sections this week, but is still inclined to play with the younger children.	No change.
Week 4	
Same as above; no change.	No change.

Example of a child study (continued).

Pre-school assessment

Section: Nine

Interest

Week 1 Nursery	Home
Martha is capable of involving herself in a particular task and seeing it through to the end. This is true of most things, unless it involves something that she dislikes. In these cases Martha tends to do a vanishing act. If Martha has any trouble with a task she asks for help, never giving up and walking away owing to lack of ability.	Attention span is variable at home. Likes to help with chores indoors, helping mum.
Week 2	
No change.	No change.
Week 3	
No change.	No change.
Week 4	
No change.	No change.

Example of a child study (continued).

Pre-school assessment

Section: Ten

Spontaneous affection

Week 1 Nursery	Home
There has been no indication of spontaneous affection towards the adults in the nursery, but Martha does cuddle the younger children.	Martha always comes up and gives her parents hugs and cuddles out of the blue. Younger children and babies very rarely escape Martha's attention for very long. All babies that visit her family get cuddles and a kiss.
Week 2	
No change.	No change.
Week 3	
No change.	No change.
Week 4	
Nothing to report.	No change.

Example of a child study (continued).

Pre-school assessment

Section: Eleven

'Good things in life'

Week 1 Nursery	Home
Martha never misses a chance to play with her friends, and seems to enjoy all special occasions. On Friday we went to the park, as we do most Fridays. Martha likes this.	Enjoys days out, playing with others. Martha does not go out much, but likes anything that is different. Hates spiders and flying insects, especially wasps and bees. However, this will not stop her enjoyment.
Week 2	
No change.	Nothing to report.
Week 3	
No change.	No change.
Week 4	
No change.	No change.

Example of a child study (continued).

Observation (Child study): Martha
Interpretation

Martha is an only child of average height and weight. She has red hair and green eyes. She speaks with a slight Irish accent. Martha's mother was very co-operative and gave me all the information about Martha's behaviour at home. I am most grateful.

I identified no areas of concern. Martha is a happy-go-lucky child who fits in well in the nursery group. Her sleeping pattern is irregular. However, she rarely seems affected by lack of sleep. She eats well and is willing to try new foods. Her bed wetting which, according to Geraghty (1988) can occur in this age group, does not appear to upset her or her mother, and she never had an accident in the nursery during the day.

Emotionally, Martha appears to be well-adjusted, displaying a full range of emotions. The occasional temper tantrum is expected at her age (Chazan et al., 1983). Any behaviour problems which her mother reported her having at one stage seem to have disappeared. She rarely displays spontaneous affection towards adults other than her immediate family, but she kisses and cuddles all babies and younger children.

She enjoys all the play activities at the nursery and at home and joins in with great enjoyment. She responds well to new challenges. She enjoys all outings and special occasions. She perseveres well at the nursery, asking for help if she cannot manage on her own. She is inquisitive and asks appropriate questions. She accepts authority well, although may question rules at home. She gets on well with her peers, showing love and concern for younger children. She can play alone as well as with her peers.

In general, Martha is a happy, average 4-year-old showing the stage of development outlined by Sheridan (1997) and College handouts.

Personal learning

I learned a great deal from this observation, especially from having such close links with Martha's parents. This gave me a very good insight into this child's behaviour and has given me a better understanding of 4-year-olds in general.

Recommendations

As Martha will be moving into the reception class in the school in the near future, she needs to be encouraged to persevere in some of the tasks she is not keen to do at the moment, such as practising writing her name and using the scissors with ease. There is some concern that Martha may find the change of teacher hard to deal with in the infant school, so it might be a good idea if she spends the occasional afternoon in the new class next term.

Bibliography

Chazan et al., 1983, *Helping Young Children with Behaviour Difficulties*, Croom Helm.
Geraghty P., 1988, *Caring for Children*, Baillière Tindall.
Sheridan M., 1997, *Children's Developmental Progress from Birth to Five Years*, Routledge.
College handouts on the 4-year-old.

Supervisor's signature

T. Weaver

Example of a child study (continued).

Sociograms

These are used either to indicate one particular child's social relationships within a group, or to look at friendship patterns of all the children within a group. Sometimes this highlights the unpopularity of a particular child and may well motivate the placement to help this child to establish fruitful relationships.

Advantages

- Can show quite clearly which children are most popular within the group.
- Would indicate which children might need some help in establishing relationships with other children.
- May make you more sensitive to changes in the social structure of the group.

Disadvantages

- Relationships within the group may change from day to day.
- Too much may be read into the data.

Games encourage children's social development

Date: 14–15 October 2001

Method: Structured recording/Sociogram

Start time: 1.45 pm (Wednesday)   Finish time: 2.00 pm (Thursday)

Number of children present: Wednesday, 28/Thursday, 29

Number of adults present: 2 + student

Permission sought from: Teacher

Type of setting:

The observations are taking place in the classroom of an inner-city, multi-cultural primary school. They will be carried out during the afternoon sessions on everyone in the Year 2 class.

The observation was carried out over a period of two days.

Immediate environment:

Wednesday: This afternoon the children are having a creative art session. Some of the children are painting their models. Others on another table are making and creating models from wood. There is also a group of children making lanterns for Divali with the teacher.

Thursday: The children are sitting in their ability groups at their tables. They are writing and creating their own stories. The special needs teacher is working with the lower ability group.

Example of a sociogram.

First name(s)/initial(s) of child(ren) observed: see table

Brief description of child(ren) observed:

Ages: 6–7 Years

Gender: 12 Males, 17 Females

There is a variety and a diverse number of cultures in the class. These include Turkish, Spanish, African–Caribbean, Nigerian, South American, Chinese, Bengali, Irish and Albanian.

Aim of observation:

To observe the social developments and friendships of children between the ages of 6 and 7 years. This will be achieved by asking each child in the class who his or her best friend is.

The purpose would be to use the collected information to ascertain the stage at which the children are in relation to social development, by comparing to developmental norms. To also identify any patterns of friendships and popularity in relation to gender and culture. To then consider and recommend appropriate activities and strategies to enhance and further develop the children's social skills.

Example of a sociogram (continued).

Observation: Looking at children's friendships

Children were asked who their best friends in the class were.

Children's names	Best friends in the class
Aaron	Cressida, Freya, Dominic, Julian, Daniel, Claire
Nazmin	Sally, Freya, Sarah
Sally	Freya, Sarah, Nazmin, Rain, Jordan
Freya	Cressida, Sally, Sarah, Nazmin, Rain, Arta, Jamia
Daniel	Cressida, Freya, Dean, Julian, Alexis, Rain
Dean	Kevin, Wai Hong, Kemal, Julian, Daniel, Alexis, Freya
Arta	Sheena, Jaz, Jamia
Jamia	Arta, Cathrine, Danielle, Sheena, Jaz
Volkan	Jaz, Claire, Dominic, Arta, Jamia, Arzu, Sally, Dennis, Kemal, Julian, Dean, Wai Hong, Kevin, Aaron, Johnny, Danielle, Daniel, Tayma, Jordan, Cathrine, Kevin, Cressida, Alexis, Rain
Cressida	Freya, Dominic, Chisom, Tayma
Cathrine	Jordan, Jamia, Arta
Dominic	Cressida, Sarah, Cathrine
Dennis	Nazmin, Sheena, Danielle, Tayma, Cathrine, Daniel, Kemal, Rain, Claire, Kevin, Arta, Jamia, Wai Hong, Jordan, Dean, Freya, Sarah, Sally, Dominic, Claire, Johnny, Alexis, Julian, Jaz, Chisom, Aaron
Kemal	Dean, Kevin, Alexis, Julian
Sarah	Claire, Sally, Freya
Wai Hong	Sally, Kevin, Dean, Julian, Volkan, Alexis, Nazmin, Freya, Kemal, Tayma, Dominic, Aaron, Arta, Johnny, Chisom, Jordan
Claire	Jaz, Jordan, Wai Hong, Cathrine, Cressida, Arta, Jamia
Johnny	Alexis, Julian, Jordan, Cressida, Tayma, Daniel, Dominic
Julian	Dean, Wai Hong, Kevin, Sarah, Freya
Chisom	Cressida, Freya, Claire, Arta, Jamia, Jordan, Cathrine
Alexis	Johnny, Tayma, Wai Hong, Daniel, Aaron
Danielle	Freya, Arta, Jordan, Rain
Tayma	Chisom, Cressida, Alexis, Jaz, Dominic
Sheena	Jordan, Rain, Claire, Arzu, Sally, Arta, Jamia, Nazmin, Cathrine, Tayma, Johnny, Jaz, Cressida, Julian, Alexis, Freya, Dominic, Sarah, Dennis, Kemal
Rain	Jordan, Dominic, Claire, Kevin
Jaz	Jordan, Freya, Arta, Sheena, Jamia, Dominic
Arzu	Arta, Alexis, Sally, Jordan, Chisom, Kevin
Jordan	Sheena, Cathrine, Claire, Johnny, Tayma, Arzu, Arta, Jamia, Chisom, Julian, Dean, Wai Hong, Kevin, Kemal, Rain, Dennis
Kevin	Sally, Wai Hong, Julian, Dean, Daniel, Jordan, Rain, Jaz, Kemal, Johnny, Cressida, Sheena, Dominic, Sarah, Aaron, Arta, Volkan, Alexis, Cathrine, Claire, Tayma, Jamia, Danielle, Chisom, Arta

Example of a sociogram (continued).

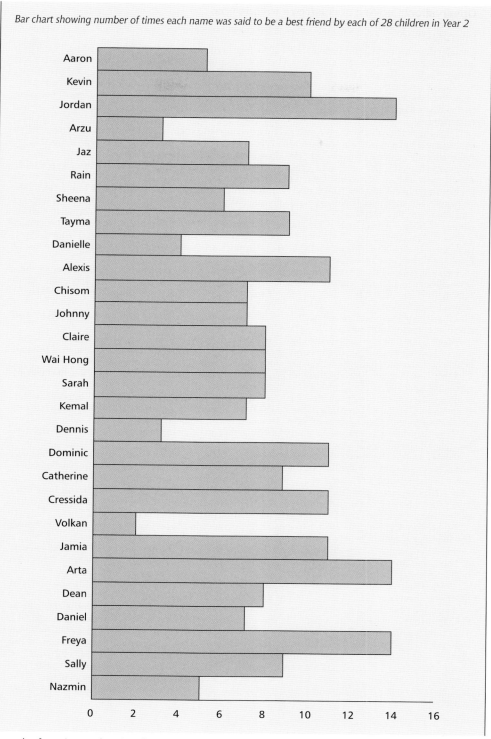

Bar chart showing number of times each name was said to be a best friend by each of 28 children in Year 2

Example of a sociogram (continued).

Observation
Sociogram: group of children
Interpretation

Social development includes the development of relationships among children and between children and adults. The socialisation process is how the children learn about their culture. The development of social skills includes sharing, taking turns and accepting rules. Bruce and Meggitt (1996) say that 'Social development includes the growth of the child's relationships with other people and socialisation, the process of learning the skills and attitudes which enable the child to live easily with other members of the community.'

The aim of this observation has been met because the social developments and friendships of children between the ages of 6 and 7 years have been observed. This was achieved by recording and asking each child in the class who his or her 'best' friend was.

From studying the table and graphs it is perceived that the children whose names were mentioned the most were Arta, Freya and Jordan (females, 14 times). The next most mentioned children were Alexis and Dominic (males, 11 times), Cressida and Jamia (females, 11 times), Kevin (male, 10 times), Rain, Tayma, Sally and Cathrine (females, 9 times), Wai Hong and Dean (males, 8 times), Claire and Sarah (females, 8 times), Kemal, Johnny and Daniel (males, 7 times), Chisom and Jaz (females, 7 times), Sheena (female, 6 times), Aaron (male, 5 times), Nazim (female, 5 times), Danielle (female, 4 times), Dennis (male, 3 times), Arzu (female, 3 times) and Volkan (male, twice). Females are mentioned more because there are 17 females in the class and only 11 males.

I was surprised that Arta was one of the names mentioned most frequently because she's been observed playing mainly with one special friend who is Jamia. Having a special friend falls within the developmental 'norms' of seven years. Hobart and Frankel (1999a) say that at seven years they have 'a special friend at school'.

However I wasn't surprised that Jordan's name was mentioned a lot because she is looked up to as a leader in the class.

More than half the girls in the class, i.e. Nazmin, Sally, Freya, Arta, Jamia, Cathrine, Sarah, Chisom, Danielle and Arzu, said only girls as their 'best' friends. Cressida, Claire and Jaz said one boy. Sixteen of the girls who were mentioned were in their literacy groups.

Only one boy, i.e. Kemal, chose all boys as his 'best' friends. Dean and Alexis said only one girl and Dominic said only girls as his 'best' friends.

It is believed that people learn the behaviour that is expected of males and females within their society. Haralambos and Holborn (1995) say that 'it is the culture of a society which exerts most influence in the creation of masculine and feminine behaviour'.

This could be a reason why many of the girls consider other girls as their 'best' friends, because of stereotyped views in society.

For example the media portrays men and women in their traditional social roles, e.g. adverts of girls playing with dolls and boys with cars, which could lead children to 'identify' with their gender. Differences are therefore emphasised which may encourage them to play with their own gender. Beaver et al. (1994) say that 'Children learn rules about how boys and girls behave from a variety of people and other influences. They learn from their adult carers, other children, and from the television and the mass media in general.'

However, dividing children into gender groups could also encourage this as this increases the likelihood of differences being emphasised.

However, many of the children, both boys and girls, mentioned a mixture of 'best' friends of the same and opposite gender (e.g. Dennis, Aaron, Jordan, Rain and Sheena). This also indicates that gender may not influence many of the children's friendships.

Being divided into groups also has an influence on the children's friendships as many of them mentioned other children in their groups as their 'best' friends.

I was surprised that when Volkan was asked who his 'best' friends were in the class, he at first said that he did not have any. Dennis encouraged him by saying that he was his friend. This falls within the developmental stage of 4–8 years, as Bruce and Meggitt (1996) say that between 4–8 years, 'They can think of the feelings of others.' Volkan then went around the class saying nearly everybody's name. During the observation only 2 children (Kevin and Wai Hong, males) had mentioned his name. Volkan is Turkish and has very limited English. This causes a language barrier which may lead to his lack of confidence when socialising. This language barrier, i.e. his limited English, may also discourage other children from socialising with him.

Example of a sociogram (continued).

The children mix with a variety of other children from a variety of cultures and races in the class. Kevin, Wai Hong and Sally are Chinese. In this observation Kevin and Wai Hong both said each other's and Sally's names first as their 'best' friends. These close friendships may be encouraged by the fact that they share the same language, culture, customs and beliefs.

Personal learning

I have learnt that bilingual children speak English at a slightly slower rate than children who are monolingual. Volkan's lack of competence in English could be an explanation for why it is difficult for him to socialise with other children as he states in the observation (until encouraged) that he doesn't have any friends.

I have gained knowledge that between the ages of 6–7 years children usually have more than one 'best' friend and will usually have a close group of friends.

I have also learnt about the importance of being a role model and providing the children with positive images. Bruce and Meggitt (1996) say that 'Discriminatory practice by children or adults that gives children negative labels of any kind, even if these are conveyed not directly to the child, but in the way that the staff talk about the child, damages social and emotional development.'

I have also learnt about the importance of providing a secure, loving environment and of encouraging the children to value themselves and so develop positive self-images and self-concepts. Bruce and Meggitt (1996) say that 'The way children are helped to believe in themselves helps them in turn to develop positive relationships with other people.'

It is believed that for this observation the written description was the most useful method for observing the children's social developments. Because a previously prepared chart with all the children's names was used this made it easier and helped me to learn their names and recognise all the children.

A disadvantage of using this method was that some of the children prompted each other to say their names which resulted in a less accurate observation. If this observation was to be repeated, the children would be asked independently in a quiet area. The book corner could be used while the rest of the class continue with set activities.

Recommendations

Additional encouragement and stimulus can now be provided to further develop the children's social skills. Future recommendations can include providing activities and games which are challenging, encouraging working in groups and promoting cooperation. Table-top activities like playing Snakes and Ladders involves cooperation, and turn-taking. Hobart and Frankel (1999b) say that 'When playing in groups, these toys and games involve turn-taking, co-operation and sharing.'

Pictures in games should reflect equal opportunities, i.e. showing pictures of people of different races, religions, cultures, genders, ages, and disabilities.

It is also important as a childcare practitioner to offer the girls equal access to physical freedom and use of large motor equipment as the boys, and to ensure girls and boys are not divided into gender groups, e.g. when queuing for lunch and saying 'all the boys can line up first' as this increases the likelihood of differences being emphasised. Because many of the girls seemed to only mention girls as their 'best' friends another recommendation could also include encouraging them and others to work with the opposite gender in groups and during paired reading. Volkan could be paired during activities with other Turkish children in the class, which may help develop his English because they can translate to him when he does not understand.

Opportunities to go on outings, for example to the zoo or to the shops, offer a wide variety of experiences. Outings are a social occasion for children, adults and parents to go out as a group. Outings provide opportunities for discussions of the environment and encourage discussions with each other. Outings need planning, and safety is a very important factor. There should be access on transport for children with disabilities. Hobart and Frankel (1999b) say that 'Outings are a great social experience, going somewhere together as a group, with children, staff and parents involved. They provide opportunities for children to talk and relate to many children, and may lead to new friendships.'

Example of a sociogram (continued).

Bibliography

Beaver M., Brewster J., Jones P., Keene A., Neaum S. and Tallack J., 1994, *Babies and Young Children, Book 1, Development 0–7*, Stanley Thornes (Publishers) Ltd.

Bruce T. and Meggitt C., 1996, *Child Care and Education* (ch. 3 p. 86, ch. 7 p. 235, ch. 7 p. 212, ch. 7 p. 224), Hodder & Stoughton.

Haralambos M. and Holborn M., 1995, *Sociology: Themes and Perspectives*, 4th edition (ch. 10 p. 589), Harper Collins Publishers.

Hobart C. and Frankel J., 1999a, *A Practical Guide to Child Observation*, 2nd edition, Nelson Thornes.

Hobart C. and Frankel J., 1999b, *A Practical Guide to Activities for Young Children*, 2nd edition, Nelson Thornes.

Supervisor's signature

L. Smith (teacher)

Example of a sociogram (continued).

Movement and flow charts

Movement and flow charts are a shorthand way of presenting information about an individual or a group of children. A movement chart might be employed to see how a child uses the establishment equipment by drawing a plan of the room and indicating by arrows the child's movement around the room.

Advantages
- Helpful in planning the use of equipment.

Disadvantages
- Of limited use.

Outdoor play

Physical development

Date: 8.1.03

Method:

> Flow chart/narrative. I chose to use the flow chart as it will enable me to record the children's movement/behaviour with ease as they move around the hall. This shorthand method will also enable me to watch and record each of the three children (and compare them), without focusing too much on the presentation of my observation. The narrative aspect of this will allow me to understand in more detail what I recorded during the session, when I refer back to it at a later date. This will also provide the reader with insight into each child's competencies and general behaviour.

Start time: 2:30   Finish time: 3:05

Number of children present: 3 (25)

Number and role of adults present:

> 0 (2). The two adults present are the teacher and myself.

Permission sought from: Supervisor

Type of setting:

> The setting is a local authority primary school, where there is a diversity of culture. This is made explicit through the various paintings and displays on walls, which challenge different stereotypes in our society.

Example of an observation using a movement/flow chart.

Immediate environment:

> It is 2:30 pm and the children have just returned to class from their afternoon break. Before they settle in, the teacher tells them to get their PE kits and line up quietly; we then make our way down to the main hall.

First name(s)/initial(s) of child(ren) observed: Y, T, Ta

Brief description of child(ren) observed:

Y is aged seven years and five months.

- She has been attending the school since her time at its nursery.
- She has one older sister aged 10 years, who also attends the school.
- Her mother is Irish and her father is Turkish.
- She is a fairly quiet child, yet seems to get along well with her peers. I also noticed that she undertakes most tasks with confidence and motivation, completing them with relative ease.

T is aged seven years and four months.

- He has been attending the school since joining its nursery.
- He has one younger sister aged five years, who also attends the school, and a younger sister aged two years.
- Both his mother and father originate from Bangladesh.
- He appears to be a generally quiet child, who during the session remained silent and simply got on with the tasks at hand. These were, however, carried out enthusiastically.

Example of an observation using a movement/flow chart (continued).

Ta is aged seven years and two months.

- She has been attending the school since joining its nursery.
- She is an only child.
- Her father is Irish and her mother is Afro-Caribbean.
- She appears to lack self-confidence in the work she engages in, talking quietly and sometimes taking quite a long time to provide answers. However, she gets along well with her peers and is generally confident amongst them.

Aim of observation:

The aim of this observation is to observe three children during a PE session, as they use the different apparatus, and how they use the space available to them, as well as looking at other aspects of their holistic development.

I want to carry out this observation in order to look at and compare the physical development of three children, as they engage in a PE session. I shall see how they each use the space available to them, and the competency shown in undertaking the various tasks during the session. Other areas of their development will also be included.

Example of an observation using a movement/flow chart (continued).

NOTE: All children followed the same activity but at slightly different times.

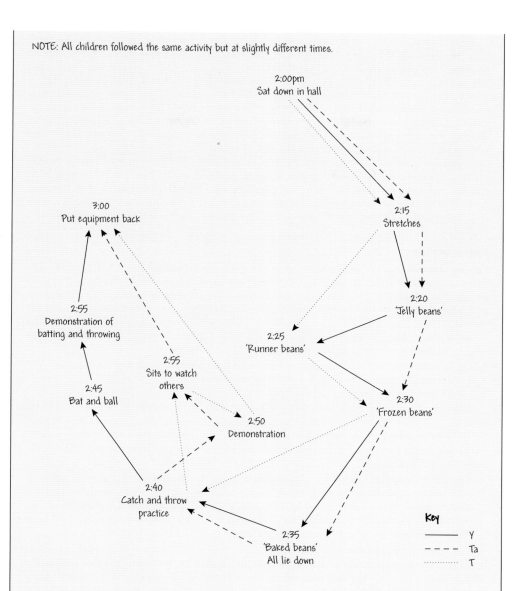

2:00pm
Sat down in hall

2:15
Stretches

3:00
Put equipment back

2:20
'Jelly beans'

2:55
Demonstration of
batting and throwing

2:25
'Runner beans'

2:55
Sits to watch
others

2:45
Bat and ball

2:50
Demonstration

2:30
'Frozen beans'

2:40
Catch and throw
practice

2:35
'Baked beans'
All lie down

Key

———— Y

– – – – Ta

·············· T

Observation

The children change into their t-shirts and shorts in the main hall and leave their belongings to the side. The teacher then calls them over and discusses what they shall be doing during the session. While she is doing so, Ta practises arm movements as Y and T watch closely. They then go straight into a warm up/stretching exercise. The teacher introduces the 'bean game' where she calls out different beans for the children to behave like: 'Runner beans!' – the children run around the hall. 'French beans!' – the children should 'Bonjour!' 'Frozen beans!' – they all freeze . . . All the children find this amusing and laugh as they follow the instructions. T makes small body movements, while Ta and Y jump around and stretch very confidently.

Example of an observation using a movement/flow chart (continued).

Roughly five minutes later, the teacher hands out tennis bats and balls to the children and they find a partner to practise their throwing skills. Ta throws the ball with both hands, almost hoisting it into the air instead of instantly releasing it. She constantly studies it as she lets go; her partner catches it successfully and Ta smiles! When it is Ta's turn to bat, she holds it very stiffly, with one hand, and misses the ball two out of three times. 'Come closer 'cos everyone's in our way!' Meanwhile T is holding the bat like a frying pan! This is held tightly up to his chest as he stands opposite but only a few small steps away from his partner. T manages to hit the ball, but when his partner stands a little further away T misses the ball and they stand talking for a few moments, until it is time to change over.

Y and her partner seem to do well. She is competent at throwing and batting, hardly missing the ball, until someone gets in the way. Y smiles as she bats the ball (using both hands), and when it is time for her to throw she uses the underarm technique with her right hand. She and her partner seem relaxed, and joke in between batting and throwing. It is now 3:00 pm and the children are asked to stop and put the equipment away, which they do efficiently.

Interpretation

Having observed each of the children, who are approximately of the same age, I can see that there is a range of ability in their development in general. For example, with regard to their physical development, Y was very confident and, competent in throwing and catching the ball, whereas Ta and T did this with more difficulty, using both hands to throw, catch and bat the ball.

According to Meggitt and Sunderland (2000, p. 102), a child of seven years should be able to

• catch and throw a ball, using one hand only
• hop on either leg, and walk along a thin line with their arms outstretched for balance
• climb on play apparatus with skill, some climbing ropes
• control speed when running and swerve to avoid collision.

However, I am aware that even amongst the same age group there will be wide variations of ability and it is unfair to label a child as being developmentally 'slow' because of this. Also, a child who manages a task better than someone else in her age range may perform 'poorer' than them in another task. It is therefore inaccurate to have narrow definitions of 'norms'. As Minnet (1985, p. 23) says:

> There *is* a recognised pattern of physical development which it is expected that children will follow, known as norms, but because there is such a wide range of normal development, it is dangerous to assume that children are abnormal if they do not all progress in exactly the same manner. Variations will always exist, since each child is an individual developing in their own unique way.

The importance of physical education within the National Curriculum must be realised, as it gives all children a chance to develop a wide range of skills, be they gross motor skills (by riding bikes, climbing apparatus), fine motor skills or social skills, and to exercise their joints/muscles. As with all the other subjects taught, physical education is also inseparable from all other aspects of development, as they are interactive and active in their learning.

> Physical development is about improving skills of coordination, control, manipulation and movement. Physical development has two other very important aspects. It helps children gain confidence in what they can do and enables them to feel the positive benefits of being healthy and active.
>
> (*Curriculum Guidance for the Foundation Stage* (2000), p. 100)

As the lesson was planned as part of the curriculum, the teacher gave out various instructions, all of which the children were listening to attentively, and later on carried out.

Throughout the observation, I also noticed that both T and Ta seemed quiet and not so confident in their movements, unlike Y who laughed and chatted as she engaged in the whole session.

Example of an observation using a movement/flow chart (continued).

It may be that these children would have benefited by some adult assistance, or even a partner who was more able than themselves, something which Lev Vygotsky refers to as the zone of proximal development (what the child can potentially do). As Bruce and Meggitt (1999, p. 179) note:

> Vygotsky believed that free play helped children to make sense of what they learn for the reason that, during this, they are free from the practical constraints of real life situations. He also believed that children have better ideas and do better thinking when an adult or child who knows more is helping them.

Although I stated that I feel T and Ta are a little under-confident, it is apparent that the teacher does treat all the children with equal respect and attention. This is of course imperative in the implementation of equality of opportunity and to further build upon the children's self-esteem, so that they too develop a positive attitude towards themselves and their potential in general, be it their physical, intellectual, language, emotional or social development. As Malik (1998, p. 52) states:

> Children need first to be given respect in order that they can then develop self-respect. Lack of access leads to poor self-esteem, lack of confidence, lack of respect, stereotyping and discrimination. Principles of good practice should therefore be foremost in the minds of adults working with young children.

The group have PE with the play apparatus every Monday, and one games session weekly. It is vital that all children get as much exercise as possible, and they should be encouraged to do so regularly, particularly those who may otherwise not have the chance. For example, those who live in high-rise accommodation may not have enough space to run around in. The school therefore plays an important part in this. Physical exercise has many advantages; some of these are identified by Bruce and Meggitt (1999, p. 131) as:

- It helps to increase bone density.
- It helps to strengthen muscles.
- It helps to strengthen joints and promotes good posture.
- Improves balance.

Exercise will also promote children's social skills and self-fulfilment, as they will be interacting and cooperating with one another, especially when they are placed in small groups – as they were today.

Meeting of stated aim

Looking back at my aim, I can see that I have achieved all that was required. That is to observe three children in a PE session, while focusing on how they use the space available to them, comparing their stages of physical development and looking at various other aspects of their holistic development.

Evaluation of selected method

Although I do feel content with this observation, I do think that I didn't observe each of the children as effectively as I could have. This is due to the fact that I had to focus on three children, while writing up a narrative description and completing the flow chart at the same time. Also, notes must be written up quickly, otherwise important details will be forgotten. There are, however, advantages to using the narrative method, these being that only a notepad and pen are needed, and that writing is a skill that we practise everyday, allows us to use our own shorthand method of recording details quickly, and also provides us with open data that can be interpreted later on. As Hobart and Frankel (1999, p. 27) state: 'The narrative method is the commonest type of observation technique, and can be used to record a naturally occurring event . . . it is a description of an event unfolding in front of you, written in present tense so that your reader can appreciate what is happening more easily.'

Example of an observation using a movement/flow chart (continued).

Using the flow chart to record the observation proved to be effective in recording details very quickly, while I focused on three children at once. This would have also proved beneficial in planning the use of PE equipment to be used. However, I feel that its disadvantages include the fact it leaves little time or room to elaborate on details, therefore not indicating the child's capabilities or behaviour.

Alternative methods that I could have used include the tick chart; this would have enabled me to record my findings efficiently and with ease. By devising my own, I could have focused on specific areas to record, thus saving much time. Its disadvantages are that the information recorded is closed; for example, although a child may have successfully completed a task, it will not indicate how easily it was achieved. Also, if a child can do more than what is recorded, it will be dismissed, as only the assessed skills are recorded.

Target child observations may also be used, which would allow me to monitor the children's progress over a continuous period of time.

Beaty (1998, p. 32) says: 'As an observer, you should step back unobtrusively and position yourself close to (but not interfering with) the children you are to observe . . . without calling attention to yourself.' This is something which I always adhere to while observing, as I do not want the child(ren) to be aware of the fact that they are being watched, as this may alter their behaviour and therefore not provide me with accurate data.

I also feel that I carried out the observation objectively, as I do not see the point in observing a child with an idea of what you already expect to be observing. The whole point of the task will be defeated, as noted by Tassoni and Beith (1999, p. 89): 'Having preconceived ideas about what the child is like, we are more likely to look and record the type of behaviour we expect, rather than the actual behaviour.'

I think that my findings are reliable, as the children's age-stage of development matches that of the textbooks that I have read. Although, 'when looking at the development of skill, it's not the age that is important, but being able to recognise the stage of development that is reached' (Athey and Balmworth (1979), p. 142).

Recommendations

To build upon what I have observed, there are various activities that can be carried out with the children, in order to move them on to their next stage of development.

> The role of the teacher is crucial in planning and providing an environment that encourages children to do things, talk about what they are doing and think about how they can improve their actions or movements. They must plan activities that offer appropriate physical challenges, while providing sufficient space, indoors and outdoors, to set up the relevant activities according to age and stage of development.
>
> (*Curriculum Guidance for the Foundation Stage* (2000), p. 101)

As stated in *A Learning Journey: A Parent's Guide to the Primary School Curriculum*, 'most schools will aim to make sure that the time children spend exercising at school – including PE and any out of hours sports – adds up to about two hours per week'. I therefore think that where possible, some more time should be given to physical activities, be it swimming, football or slightly longer PE lessons, in order to consolidate skills learnt (like teamwork and repetition of skills such as control and coordination while using equipment). In this case, tennis bats, throwing and catching.

Also of great importance is for the teacher not to make any assumptions based upon gender, regarding limitations on the child's behaviour, for example telling a boy not to cry when he hurts himself, or excluding girls from using the climbing apparatus. Children therefore need positive role models around them. As Malik (1998, p. 113) says, 'All professional childcare and education workers and teachers should avoid sex-role stereotyping of young children, and implement anti-sexist practices.'

Example of an observation using a movement/flow chart (continued).

Bibliography

A Learning Journey: A Parent's Guide to the Primary School Curriculum (2001), Department for Education and Skills.
Athey C. and Balmworth N., 1979, *The Pre-School Child*, Ward Lock.
Beaty J., 1998, *Observing Development of the Young Child*, Prentice Hall.
Bruce T. and Meggitt C., 1999, *Childcare and Education*, Hodder & Stoughton.
Curriculum Guidance for the Foundation Stage, 2000, Qualifications and Curriculum Authority.
Hobart, C. and Frankel, J., 1999, *A Practical Guide to Child Observation*, Stanley Thornes.
Malik H., 1998, *A Practical Guide to Equal Opportunities*, Stanley Thornes.
Meggitt C. and Sunderland G., 2000, *Child Development*, Heinemann.
Minnet P., 1985, *Childcare and Development*, John Murray.
Tassoni P. and Beith K., 1999, *Nursery Nursing*, Heinemann.

Supervisor's signature

A. Stephenson

Example of an observation using a movement/flow chart (continued).

Media

Photographs and video recordings

It is not necessary for students to use photographs or video recordings of children. Qualified practitioners use these techniques rarely and only with the written permission of the parents. They should be used only to demonstrate a skill, in the same way that a child's drawing might be included if qualified staff wanted to illustrate competence at an activity.

Advantages
- A statement that should stand up on its own.
- Less writing involved.

Disadvantages
- What you see may not be obvious to other people.
- Always need to obtain permission.
- Children can be recognised at a later date.
- When they are older, children might feel their rights have been infringed by using photographs of them without their permission

Taped language samples

To obtain an accurate sample of a child's speech, it is necessary to use a tape recorder in order to make sure that you have recorded everything the child has said. Before undertaking this task, you must obtain the permission of the placement and of the parent. Make sure you are familiar with the mechanics of the recorder you are going to use. Remember to identify on tape brief details of the purpose of your recording, where you are and who you are with. The tape would then be included in your observation portfolio, with or without a transcript. You will need to write an evaluation of the taped language. The tapes may be used for children who are thought to have a language delay or immature speech and can be very useful as an assessment tool for a speech therapist. They could be the basis on which to assess future progress.

Speech therapists often ask for help in recording the speech of very young children as the child may not be so confident and relaxed with a stranger.

Advantages
- An accurate sample of speech is obtained.
- Helpful to colleagues and other professionals.
- Can be a key tool in referral.
- Helps to integrate the theory of language development with the practice.
- It can be helpful to play the speech sample to parents, to initiate discussion.

Disadvantages
- Difficulty in finding a tape recorder in good working order.
- Requires certain technical skills to operate the recorder.

- Doing the recording might put the child off, and inhibit language.
- Background noise may interfere with the recording.
- Could be seen as infringing a child's rights, but a transcript can be made and the tape destroyed.

Activity

What method of observation could be used for the following aims? Select the most appropriate technique for each. Give reasons for your answers.

1   The aim of the observation is to observe the fine manipulative skills of a three-year-old child during a cutting and sticking activity.

2   The aim of the observation is to observe the concentration span of a small group of three-year-old children during a free play session in the nursery.

3   The aim of the observation is to observe the listening skills of a five-year-old child during a storytelling session in school.

4   The aim of the observation is to observe the social development of a four-year-old child during a free play session.

5   The aim of the observation is to assess the physical skills of a two-year-old child in relation to the 'norms'.

6   The aim of the observation is to observe the behaviour of a three-year-old child throughout the morning in the nursery.

7   The aim of the observation is to observe the writing skills of a six-year-old child.

8   The aim of the observation is to observe the behaviour of a small group of seven-year-old children in the school playground.

9   The aim of the observation is to observe the gross manipulative skills of a two-year-old baby in the park.

10 The aim of the observation is to observe a one-year-old child communicating with the carer in the childminder's home.

© Alison Mitchell

The High/Scope technique

There are numerous ways of assessing children, using all types of tests and charts. High/Scope uses an ongoing type of assessment, noting progress in the development of each child over a three-month period.

High/Scope Pre-school Key Experiences

Creative Representation

- Recognizing objects by sight, sound, touch, taste, and smell
- Imitating actions and sounds
- Relating pictures, photographs, and models to real places and things
- Pretending and role-playing
- Making models out of clay, blocks, etc.
- Drawing and painting

Social Relations/Initiative

- Making and expressing choices, plans and decisions
- Solving problems encountered in play
- Taking care of one's own needs
- Expressing feelings in words
- Participating in group routines
- Being sensitive to the feelings, interests, and needs of others
- Building relationships with children and adults
- Creating and experiencing collaborative play
- Dealing with social conflict in constructive ways

Language and Literacy

- Talking with others about personally meaningful experiences
- Describing objects, events, and relations
- Having fun with language: listening to stories and poems, making up stories and rhymes
- Writing in various ways: drawing, scribbling, letter-like forms, invented spelling, conventional forms
- Reading in various ways: reading storybooks, signs, symbols and other print materials

Movement

- Moving in place
- Moving from place to place
- Moving with objects
- Describing movement
- Interpreting movement directions
- Expressing creativity in movement
- Feeling and expressing beat
- Moving with others to a common beat

A Practical Guide to Child Observation and Assessment

Music

- Responding to music
- Making and describing sounds
- Playing musical instruments
- Singing

Classification

- Exploring and describing similarities, differences and the attributes of things
- Sorting and matching
- Using and describing something in several different ways
- Distinguishing between "some" and "all"
- Holding more than one attribute in mind at a time
- Describing characteristics something does not possess or what class it does not belong to

Seriation

- Comparing attributes: longer/shorter; rougher/smoother, etc.
- Arranging several things one after another in a series or pattern and describing the relationships: big, bigger, biggest
- Fitting one ordered set of objects to another through trial and error

Number

- Comparing number and amount to determine "more", "less", "fewer", "same amount"
- Arranging two sets of objects in one-to-one correspondence
- Counting objects as well as counting by rote

Space

- Filling and emptying
- Fitting things together and taking them apart
- Changing the shape and arrangement of objects (folding, twisting, stretching, stacking)
- Observing things and places from different spatial viewpoints
- Experiencing and describing relative positions, directions and distances of things in the immediate environment (play space, building, neighbourhood)
- Interpreting spatial relations in drawings, pictures, and photographs

Time

- Starting and stopping an action on signal
- Experiencing and describing different rates of movement
- Experiencing and comparing time intervals
- Experiencing and anticipating change and sequences of events.

HIGH/SCOPE KEY EXPERIENCE NOTES – KEY EXPERIENCES FOR CHILDREN AGE 3 TO 5

Child's Name:

Remember to date all entries

Language and literacy	Creative representation	Classification	Seriation ordering	Space	Number	Time	Movement	Music	Soc. relations/ Initiative

For more information about High/Scope Curriculum and key experiences contact High/Scope UK, 192 Maple Road, London SE20 8HT. Tel. 020 8676 0220, e-mail highscope@btconnect.com, web www.high-scope.org.uk

High/Scope Endorsed Trainer   Key Experience Notes (K.E.N.)   (Condensed Sheet)

Child's Name: Jinnie   Birth Date: 16/9/86   (Remember to date all entries)

LANGUAGE AND LITERACY	CREATIVE REPRESENTATION	CLASSIFICATION	SERIATION	NUMBER
5/9/91:- J was sitting looking at a story book and telling a story from the pictures	2/9/91:- Playing with the plastic animals and making the appropriate sounds for horse, cow and pig	7/10/91:- Stacked up the brick piles into separate colours - red, blue, green and yellow	11/91:- Remarked that the new fruit bowl was heavier than the old one	18/9/91:- Said "a few means not a lot"
3/9/91:- Said "Go Jo Flow Blow - they sound the same"	24/9/91:- Nailed two pieces of wood together in a cross shape and said it was an aeroplane	12/11/91:- Said "My boots are red and yours are blue"	27/9/91 :- Comparing paint brushes said "Mine's larger and fatter that yours"	18/11/91:- Cut dough into four pieces and said "I've made four cakes"
3/12/91:- Whilst sitting on a toilet seat said that she was sitting on an "O"	8/11/91:- Drew a robin with minute details and coloured it in accurately with red	6/12/91:- Looking at the words "Jack" and "Jake" said that the two names were nearly the same, just a little bit different	17/12/91:- Chose a number of triangle shapes from the box and arranged them in order of increasing size	6/12/91:- Counted 7 penguins accurately on a friend's jumper

SPACE	TIME	MUSIC AND MOVEMENT*	SOCIAL RELATIONS/INITIATIVE
23/9/91:- Talking to another child about a hat said "You need the ribbons at the back, not the side"	8/10/91:- When the tidy-up sound was made, J began to put things from the floor into their correct basket	12/9/91:- Was walking around the nursery on all fours swaying from side to side being an elephant	4/10/91:- On coming from the garden to the inside. stopped in the doorway to leave muddy wellingtons outside
30/10/91:- Folded a piece of card in half to form a tunnel and then walked plastic animals through it and used the word through	28/11/91:- Said "If you want to find me later, I'll be in the Book Area"	21/10/91:- For the first time managed to use her legs to make the swing go	29/10/91:- Took a friend into the bathroom and used a cotton wool ball to wipe mud from his knee
9/12/91:- Noticed a triangular patch of light on the carpet and found a triangle shape to fit exactly on top of it	29/11/91:- Looked at a list of names on the board and said "It will be Matthew's turn to open the door tomorrow"	13/12/91:- Used scissors to cut a "fringe" along the side of a piece of paper	12/12/91:- At snack time said "G only likes bananas - please save one for him"

*Music and Movement have since been separated into 2 categories.

6 Recording observations and assessments of various age groups

This chapter covers:

- Babies and toddlers: 0–3 years
- Foundation Stage: 3–6 years
- Infant school: 6–8 years
- Child protection

Learning outcomes

During your training you will be working with different age groups, in various settings. Some methods of observation and assessment are designed for particular age groups. The Ofsted Registration and Inspection framework requires all establishments to set up and maintain a framework for observation and assessment. Observations play an important part in recognition of abuse or neglect, and all childcare practitioners and students should be aware of the guidelines and procedures that will enable them to carry out the policies for protecting children in their establishments.

Babies and toddlers: 0–3 years

Many of you, prior to your training, may not have had much contact with small babies because of the reduction in family size and increased social mobility. You may find that working with babies really interests you, and many centres suggest that you should make contact with a friend or neighbour who has a small baby and visit regularly so as to observe mother and baby interaction.

Activity

After your visits to a mother and baby ask yourself the following questions:

In what ways did the baby express her needs?

What needs did you identify?

How did the mother respond?

Did the mother immediately know what the baby wanted?

Could the mother predict what the baby needed?

Was the mother playing with and talking to the baby?

What activities would you recommend to extend the development of the baby?

As with any observation of any age group, it is useful to observe babies and children when you first have contact with them, so that you have a baseline with which to compare any further more detailed observations and assessments.

Once you are working with babies you will need to follow the SureStart framework for effective practice 'Birth to three matters'. If you are training in an establishment that has babies, you should ask to see this pack.

Solitary play

Snapshot observation

Name: Date:

Date of birth: Starting date:

Age:

	Describe
Home language	
Other language	
Place in family	
Physical description	
Physical skills	
Advanced in areas of development	
Social skills	
Toilet trained	
Language skills	
Delays in areas of development	

You may photocopy this sheet for your own use. © *Nelson Thornes Ltd.*

A Practical Guide to Child Observation and Assessment

The treasure basket

Once the baby is sitting with support, one interesting activity you might like to carry out and observe is watching a baby using a treasure basket, as described by Elinor Goldschmied.

The baby is offered a container filled with objects made of natural materials, and chosen for their interesting shape as well as texture. About twenty items are needed to stimulate the five senses, such as a baby mirror, an orange, a fir cone, a piece of pumice, a small natural sponge, tissue paper, small cloth bags containing lavender or cloves, a brush, a piece of velvet, clothes pegs and a bunch of keys. All the equipment needs to be kept clean, and perishable objects such as fruit need to be discarded and replaced as necessary. Select items that have no sharp edges. Do not put in any items that are small enough to be inserted into noses or ears. A comfortable and safe position for the baby must be found, so that she does not topple over and become distracted. She should be allowed to explore the items on her own. You should observe her from a distance and not talk or interact with her as she plays and explores, as this will interfere with her concentration. You need to be alert to when she becomes bored, or has had enough.

Heuristic play

This type of play was also devised by Elinor Goldschmied for groups of toddlers and is particularly suitable for children in day care. It is intended as an enrichment of the children's play and the staff have to be committed to carrying it out on a regular basis.

Fifteen bags need to be provided and each bag should have enough of the same objects for all the children in the group. The contents might include bulldog clips, corks, springs, curlers, short pieces of chain, old keys, cardboard tubes, extra-large curtain rings, tins and lids, small boxes and anything else that a toddler would safely enjoy exploring. Receptacles should be provided for the children to collect the object in.

The role of the adults is to provide the objects and keep them clean and in good order. They should not participate in the play in any way, but just sit quietly at the side of the room, which has been emptied of all furniture and equipment. The children enter this empty space and start exploring the objects in the bags. The activity can go on for 40 minutes, thoroughly engrossing the children in the same way that the treasure basket does for babies. Toddlers have an increasing desire to explore and experiment and heuristic play satisfies this need. This activity will allow you to observe the development of the children and many interesting observations may be recorded.

Longitudinal baby observations

The following baby study outline has been provided by Margaret O'Donovan.

Your baby observations are a valuable and vitally important part of your course. As a qualified childcare and education practitioner you will be expected to have a sound knowledge of the health and development of babies, backed up by practical experience, as well as being conversant with all aspects of baby care.

During your training, your experience with young babies may be limited. It is, therefore, essential that you make full use of the opportunities afforded you by closely observing one particular baby. Your observations should reflect the baby's progress in the following areas:

1 **Motor development:** head control, rolling over, sitting, crawling, standing, furniture walking, walking
2 **Hand–eye coordination/manipulative skills:** development of vision, grasping rattle, hand regard, reaching for objects, grasping cube, transfer of objects, immature and mature pincer grip
3 **Hearing and language development:** response to sounds of differing pitch and loudness, turning to sound, locating sounds, development of sounds, e.g. 'a', 'm', 'b' through to first meaningful words, babbling, gurgling
4 **Social development:** smiling, recognising familiar people, e.g. parents and siblings, shyness with strangers, bathtime, feeding, weaning, finger feeding, drinking from cup.

Baby observations should be carried out at least every two weeks and always by prior arrangement with the parent. Your observations should always begin with the baby's first name, age, date and title of the observation.

In addition to the developmental observations there are health screening checks/assessments which you are advised to make every effort to attend. It is the responsibility of each student to make the necessary arrangements with the baby's parent for attendance at these check-ups. These examinations and assessments will include the following:

1 A medical examination and assessment at 6 weeks. Watch particularly for the testing of the primitive reflexes and the examination for congenital dislocation of the hip (CDH).
2 Hearing distraction test at 7 to 8 months. Permission from the health visitor will be needed to observe this test.
3 Possible developmental assessment at 9 months and/or 12 months according to the policy of the general practitioner or child health clinic.

It is also advisable that you attend at least one immunisation session. Details of illnesses or operations should be included in your observations.

Illness develops faster in a baby than in an older child, and any disease can progress quickly, in some cases becoming life threatening. If you are at all worried about the baby, you should contact the parents as soon as possible at an early stage, and then, with their permission, telephone the doctor. Signs of ill health to cause concern are:

- refusal to feed over several feeds
- a rise or fall in temperature
- noisy or laboured breathing
- convulsions or fits
- excessive crying that continues despite cuddles and feeds
- sunken or bulging anterior fontanelle (the soft spot on the crown of the head)
- a rash
- a persistent cough
- discharge from the ears, or if the baby pulls on the ears and cries
- changes in the stools or urine
- a very quiet, pale baby, difficult to rouse, and refusing to feed
- vomiting and diarrhoea
- poor muscle tension (the baby is very 'floppy').

Percentile charts

Percentile charts are used for recording the weight, height and head circumference of babies and children. There are separate charts for boys and girls, which were compiled after taking the measurements of thousands of children.

The thick line labelled 50th on the chart overleaf is the average measurement. The line marked 99.6th shows weights of girls who are heaviest in their group. As you record a measurement regularly on a chart the line will show you the child's individual progress, and allow you to compare that child with other children.

Foundation Stage: 3–6 years

The Foundation Stage Curriculum begins when children reach the age of three years, as most children of this age attend some form of pre-school or nursery provision, either full or part time. The curriculum is based on the six Early Learning Goals:

- personal, social and emotional development
- communication, language and literacy
- mathematical development
- knowledge and understanding of the world
- physical development
- creative development.

The last year of the Foundation Stage is often the reception year of an infant or primary school. The Foundation Stage Profile is based on the continuous

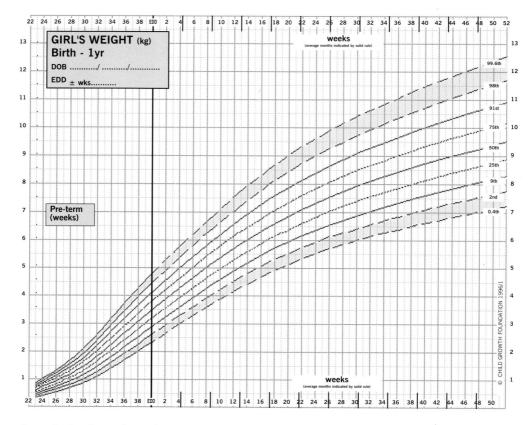

22 24 26 28 30 32 34 36 38 EDD 2 4 6 8 10 12 14 16 18 20 22 24 26 28 30 32 34 36 38 40 42 44 46 48 50 52

13

GIRL'S WEIGHT (kg)
Birth - 1yr

DOB ..../............/............

EDD ± wks...........

weeks
(average months indicated by solid rule)

99.6th
98th
91st
75th
50th
25th
9th
2nd
0.4th

Pre-term
(weeks)

CHILD GROWTH FOUNDATION 1996/1

weeks
(average months indicated by solid rule)

22 24 26 28 30 32 34 36 38 EDD 2 4 6 8 10 12 14 16 18 20 22 24 26 28 30 32 34 36 38 40 42 44 46 48 50

Percentile chart for a girl's weight (© Child Growth Foundation)

observation and assessment of all areas of the early years curriculum. Practitioners are required to observe children and respond appropriately to help them make progress. They should

- make systematic observations and assessments of each child's achievements, interests and learning styles
- use these observations and assessments to identify learning priorities and plan relevant and motivating learning experiences for each child
- match their observations to the expectations of the Early Learning Goals.

Some observations will have been carefully planned, whilst others will occur spontaneously. Some nurseries collect spontaneous observations of children by recording what they see on Post-it notes, and then transferring these on to a sheet, adding them later to the Foundation Stage Profile. Your establishment will have a copy of the Foundation Stage Profile Handbook, and you will need to spend some time studying it. Practitioners have generally welcomed the fact that continuous observation and assessment rather than tasks and tests are the basis for the scheme, and that parents are fully involved in the process.

Personal, social and emotional development

Dispositions and attitudes

✓ circle if alternative assessment applies

1 Shows an interest in classroom activities through observation or participation.

2 Dresses, undresses and manages own personal hygiene with adult support.

3 Displays high levels of involvement in self-chosen activities.

4 Dresses and undresses independently and manages own personal hygiene.

5 Selects and uses activities and resources independently.

6 Continues to be interested, motivated and excited to learn.

7 Is confident to try new activities, initiate ideas and speak in a familiar group.

8 Maintains attention and concentrates.

9 Sustains involvement and perseveres, particularly when trying to solve a problem or reach a satisfactory conclusion.

✓ circle if further assessment applies

COMMENTS

● Autumn term
● Spring term
● Summer term

Points 4 to 8 are derived from the early learning goals and can be achieved in any order.

Personal, social and emotional development

Social development

✓ circle if alternative assessment applies

1 Plays alongside others.

2 Builds relationships through gesture and talk.

3 Takes turns and shares with adult support.

4 Works as part of a group or class, taking turns and sharing fairly.

5 Forms good relationships with adults and peers.

6 Understands that there need to be agreed values and codes of behaviour for groups of people, including adults and children, to work together harmoniously.

7 Understands that people have different needs, views, cultures and beliefs that need to be treated with respect.

8 Understands that s/he can expect others to treat her or his needs, views, cultures and beliefs with respect.

9 Takes into account the ideas of others.

✓ circle if further assessment applies

COMMENTS

● Autumn term
● Spring term
● Summer term

Points 4 to 8 are derived from the early learning goals and can be achieved in any order.

3

Theo   3/10
On two wheeled trike able to keep balance. Freewheels pushing with his feet, doesn't pedal
—
Kicks ball with R/foot
Strong kick

Theo   8/10
Looking at the photographs of animals.
"Look there's a Lioness. She's like La La" (Lioness from the Lion King).
"There's no lioness here", pointing to animals

Theo   10/10
Concentrated well and persevered painting a big box in the garden covering all the areas. "I'm going to stand inside later". "I can make a racing car." He then heard the wind chimes. "I can have a church". I pointed out the wind chimes. He then made a connection with Cinderella saying "She had to run out of the palace, her clothes changed."

Theo   6/11 am   Woodwork
"My daddy's got a hammer at home and now I'm using a real one." Holds nail with left hand and hammers with right. Hammers nail right in.
"What's that?" – points to ruler. Measures out where he wants to cut wood. Saws along line.
"What's that?" – points to pinchers. "My mum uses them on the trees in the garden".

Theo   18/11 am
Comes to toothpaste activity. Uses both index fingers to make pattern. Asks for more paint. Uses back of fork to make pattern. Mixes two colours together.

Theo   21/1 am   Red Room
Draws on paper and then wants to put rubber bands around paper. Help him to roll paper. He stretches the band over top and rolls it to middle. Does the same either end. Uses tape to stick edges where bands are not there. Uses glue stick over tape. Theo spent about 20 mins doing this.

Theo   9/12 am
"Where's Nisa?" Ask Theo who he is looking for. "Nisa – she's my friend – my very best friend".
(Anisa)

Theo   3/12/02
T: "Why do reindeer have horns?"
A: "For protection from other animals . To help them keep out of danger."
T: "To keep the buffalo off their babies?"   K&U

Example of Post-it notes and associated chart

Theo

Term 1	Significant developments	Developmental needs and strategies	Review dates	Parents' consultations	Other agencies
	autumn '02				
Personal, social and emotional	Settled easily, ran in staff room 2nd day. Hears Jessica call Puja, approaches her and speaks to her (confident for a new child) Chats to George K, asks "how are you today?" 21.11 Initiates activity (i.e. rolling balls down guttering fixed to board) 9.12 – Seeks out others. 3.10.2 – asking q's				
Communication, language and literacy	9.10.2 – Mark making 10.10.2 – recalling detail of familiar story 30.10 – recog letters in name 6.11.2 – retells familiar story. Asked reg. no of his jeep, says ABCD 21.11.2 – has fav. story 3.12.2 – asking q's/reasoning				
Mathematical development	Sorts dinos by col. and names cols/shapes – shows me △ ▢ ○ ▢ and names △ Makes connections ◇ "like a kite", ○ "like a baloon". Playing with striped ball ⊚ says it's a beach ball – matching pattern Pattern making 18.11.2 Counts Ch in staffroom (✓)				
Knowledge and understanding	Asking q's and exploring water tray. Bends twig in sand ⌒ "Look I made a bridge" 8.10 – interested in animal photos 18.11.2 Investigating equipment 6.11.2 – exploring flour/water weather: "it's darker and darker … let's hope no thunder comes". Stands under leaky roof. "It's a shower". 6.11.2 exploring tools and making connections to home experience. Shows adult space pics on wall. "These are planets." Connections – adult suggests looking for buried treasure and he says "you find clues"				
Physical development	2.10.2 – good ball skills. + 7.12.2 (noticed by all staff) 3.10 – Managing tweezer Uses rope ladder, A frames and tunnel very confidently Practising throwing/catching with beanbag				
Creative development	10.10 – Painting outside Danced in garden with Natasha, followed her instructions e.g. spinning/running on the spot. 21.11.2 – exploring equipment in CLL area. Taped, singing Twinkle Twinkle				

Example of Post-it notes and associated chart (continued).

Creative activity

Activity

What framework of observation and assessment is used in your establishment to complete the Profile in the reception class?

Infant school: 6–8 years

Once children reach Year 1 of the Infant School, at the age of six years, they will follow the National Curriculum, leading to standard assessment tasks at the end of Key Stage 1. Observations tend to be informal as assessment becomes more formal, pupils receiving grades for work and school reports written once or twice a year.

The Piaget conservation test

A test you might like to carry out in the infant school is a Piaget conservation test. These are ways of testing mathematical concepts in young children and quite often have surprising results.

According to Piaget, children of five or six years of age cannot conserve. This means that their thought processes are dominated by the appearances of things, and they do not realise that the volume of an object may not change just because the appearance changes. Conservation occurs when children are able to take in several features of the objects they are looking at all at the same time.

You must be careful to be neutral and objective when administering these tests and be sure to praise the child whatever the answer.

Conservation of number

Show a child two rows of buttons, and ask him or her to count each row. When he or she has agreed that there is the same number in both rows, spread one row of buttons out. Then ask if either of the two rows contains more buttons. A child who cannot conserve will say that the spread out row must have more buttons.

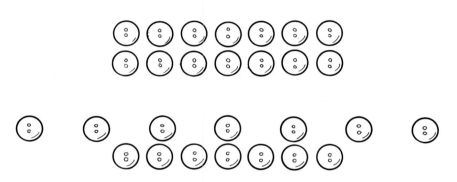

Conservation of mass

Show the child two balls of clay and get his or her agreement that both balls contain the same amount of clay. Then roll one of the balls into a sausage shape and ask the child if they still contain the same amount of clay. A child who cannot conserve will say that the sausage shape must contain more than the other ball, as it looks as if it contains more.

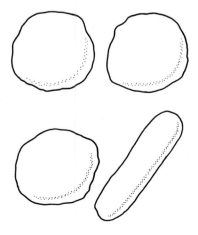

Conservation of volume

Ask the child to pour water into two identical tall thin jars until the child is satisfied that both contain an equal amount. Then, in front of the child, pour the water from one of the jars into a shorter but wider jug. A child who cannot conserve will say the tall jar contains more liquid.

Children enjoy working with numbers

Cognitive development

Date: 4.2.03

Method: Checklist and Piaget's conservation tests

Start time: 2:30   Finish time: 3:00

Number of children present: Whole class

Number and role of adults present: 1 teacher, 1 student

Permission sought from: Supervisor

Type of setting: Infant school

Immediate environment:

Large open classroom

First name(s)/initial(s) of child(ren) observed: Y, J, S, K

Brief description of child(ren) observed:

Ages: Y: 4:0, J: 4:0, S: 5:11, K: 6:2

Gender: Y and J: Male, S and K: Female

Aim of observation:

To observe children's cognitive responses to Piaget's

conservation tests for number, mass and volume.

Example of an observation using a checklist and Piaget's conservation tests.

Table to show whether children are able to conserve in three areas of maths

	Volume				Mass				Number			
	Yes	No	Yes	No	Yes	No	Yes	No	Yes	No	Yes	No
Reception												
J	✓			✓	✓			✓	✓			✓
Y	✓			✓	✓			✓	✓		✓	
Year 1												
S	✓			✓	✓			✓	✓		✓	
K	✓			✓	✓			✓	✓		✓	

Observation

I set out the texts described below for each child individually. I started with the reception class, first J and then Y. To start with I asked them if the things were the same, and then after I had changed their appearance I asked if they were still the same. I then did this with S and K in Year 1.

I then completed a checklist of their answers. The first 'yes' and 'no' in the table under each area shows whether the children agreed that it was the same at the beginning. The second shows whether they still thought it was the same or not after I had changed its appearance.

Number

The child is shown two identical lines of counters. Then one line is spaced out in front of the child. The child is then asked if there are still the same number of counters. Children who can conserve know that as nothing has been taken away the same amount is still there.

Example of an observation using a checklist and Piaget's conservation tests (continued).

A Practical Guide to Child Observation and Assessment

Mass

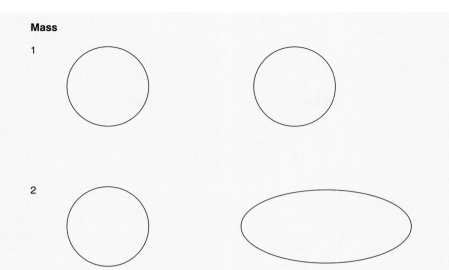

1

2

The child is shown two identical balls of dough. Then one piece of dough is flattened or rolled into a sausage shape in front of the child. The child is then asked if they are still the same. A child who can conserve understands that the amount of dough is still the same, but the shape has changed.

Volume

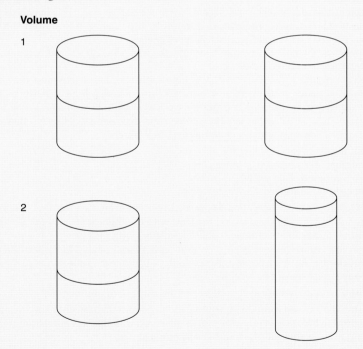

1

2

The child is shown two identical beakers with the same amount of drink in them. One of the drinks is poured into a taller beaker in front of the child. The child is then asked if there is any difference in the amount of drink. Children who can conserve know that there is still the same amount of drink.

Example of an observation using a checklist and Piaget's conservation tests (continued).

When I began doing the observation and I picked two children to come and do it with me, all the children said 'Can I do it too?'

During the observation in both reception and Year 1 class a lot of the children did not understand my original question so in some cases I had to rephrase it in simpler words. To begin with I said to one of the children, 'Is there the same amount in each glass?' The child just looked at me and said she did not know, so I changed the question very slightly and she understood it better. I said to her, 'Are the two glasses the same?' She understood me better and said no.

The same happened with some of the other questions I asked. However, I did not rephrase the question to make the answer easier, but just so that they understood what I was asking them for.

Interpretation

From my observation I have found out that most of the children were unable to conserve but that three of the children I asked were able to conserve with number. They were able to see that in each line even though the gaps were bigger there were the same number of counters.

Although most of the children whom I tested were unable to conserve, this is in line with Piaget, who suggested that most children under the age of six would not be able to conserve. All the children I observed were under the age of six, although many psychologists have found that younger children are able to conserve.

Piaget's ideas about the stages of development that children go through have influenced the way young children are taught, although other theorists have criticised aspects of his work.

It is thought that the suggested ages of the stages are underestimated. Tests by others have found that children can conserve and decentre at much earlier ages. This may be because the way the question is worded could make a difference; also the question should only be asked once because otherwise the child would feel more confused.

Other theorists, such as Bruner, believe that the idea of stages is not accurate and that children's learning is an ongoing process.

Piaget says cognitive development develops with age. He discovered that children's answers to intelligence tests were not random but followed logical patterns based on conclusions drawn from their own experiences. Piaget called these *schemas* and said that children adapt their schemas when they have new experiences. He says there are four cognitive stages of learning which a child has to pass through:

- sensory motor (0–2 years)
- pre-operational (2–7 years)
- concrete-operational (7–11 years)
- formal thought (11–adult).

When I was doing my observation I observed four children, two from reception and two from Year 1, and in both the classes I did the tests with the highest and lowest ability child. In both classes the higher ability child was able to conserve with number.

As I observed children from both reception and Year 1, I have looked at the norms of cognitive development for a four and six year old. Meggitt and Sunderland (2000) say that at the age of four a child should be able to:

- Enjoy counting up to twenty and understand the concept of number

The children I observed from this age range did not count up to twenty and the most I have seen them count to before was ten. One child I observed was able to understand the concepts of number up to six as this was the number of counters I had.

- Sort objects into groups

I had different coloured counters for the number test, and one of the children from reception started putting the counters in order of colour.

- Give reasons and solve problems

Example of an observation using a checklist and Piaget's conservation tests (continued).

The children from reception that I observed were unable to give reasons, as when I asked why at one point the child just looked blankly at me.

• Have increased memory skill

I have not proved this long term but when I went to Year 1 the next day one of the children whom I had observed the day before said 'Are you going to do that thing which you did with me yesterday?'

As I observed children in Year 1 as well as reception I have looked at the norms of development for a six year old, as outlined by Meggitt and Sunderland (2000):

• Children begin to think in a more co-ordinated way, and can hold more than one point of view at a time.

The children I observed in Year 1 both thought hard about each question before giving me their answer.

• Begin to develop concepts of quantity, length, measurement, distance, area, time, volume, capacity and weight.

In the areas covered by the observation the children were not able to understand the concept of conservation of number, mass and volume.

An important point to consider when testing the children is the child's confidence. If the child lacks confidence then they are likely to say the least possible; they might think that saying yes would lead them to answer further questions but if they said no they might not have to. Also the child may not even say anything, which may suggest to the adult that they either do not know the answer or do not understand the question.

The child will need to have a wide range of language in order to understand and respond to the questions I have asked. Also the child's concentration can affect their responses: if they are not really concentrating maybe it is because they are particularly tired or hungry; then they are less likely to conserve.

Personal learning

I have learnt quite a lot from my observation. For example, I have learnt that children seem to concentrate when they are taken out on their own and they listen well. Piaget says that most children under the age of six are unable to conserve but in my observation two children were able to conserve with number, which surprised me.

How I ask the questions is important, and I have to make sure the child understands what I am asking them to do.

In considering anti-discriminatory or anti-bias practice, I would make sure that I did not single out any particular child. If one child was able to conserve whilst another was not, I would not tell either of them that they were right or wrong, but I would be pleased with both for their answers. I would not always pick the same child to praise. I would give more help to a child if it was needed because they had a particular problem, but I would try and make sure that none of the other children who did not need extra help felt that I was favouring the child or children that I was helping.

Evaluation

By using a checklist method I was able to observe the children easily. Because the checklist was very precise I was able to note easily what the children said, and I was able to easily compare this to the normal stages of a child's development.

If I had more time I could have observed all the children. This would have been better because the children I did test wanted to know what they were doing. If all the children were doing the tests, those that I did test may have had more confidence because everyone was doing the same thing.

Example of an observation using a checklist and Piaget's conservation tests (continued).

Recommendations

To help improve a child's cognitive development it is important to provide opportunities to improve it. For example, provide opportunities to talk about number and language, and to give encouragement to the child. Toys and games are also important and should be chosen to encourage children to sort, group, remember and recall information. Matching games may also help.

Bibliography

Beaver M. et al., 2001, *Babies and Young Children, Diploma in Child Care and Education*, Nelson Thornes (pp. 133–4).
Meggitt C. and Sunderland G., 2000, *Child Development: An Illustrated Guide*, Heinemann (pp. 77–91).
Brennand H. et al., 2001, *Child Development*, Hodder Arnold (pp. 306–15).
Flanagan C., 2000, *A Level Psychology*, Letts Educational (pp. 201–4, 212–13).
Woods, B., 2000, *Basics in Psychology*, Hodder & Stoughton Educational (pp. 181–9).
Tassoni, P. et al., 2002, *Diploma in Child Care and Education*, Heinemann Educational (pp. 194–206).

Supervisor's signature

C. Knight

Example of an observation using a checklist and Piaget's conservation tests (continued).

Child protection

When you are still training, you might be concerned about one of the children in the establishment. You should alert your supervisor immediately, who will initiate the correct procedures, following the child protection policy outlined by the Area Protection Committee. Your supervisor might request that you record your observations in writing.

Once you have qualified, if you notice any physical signs of abuse, for example bruises or burns that are revealed during PE or rest sessions, or when changing a nappy, you must make a written, dated and timed note of the facts immediately, as if they are not written within 24 hours they are not legally admissible. It would be advisable to ask another professional adult to confirm your findings discreetly. You should then report the matter at once to your manager or designated teacher, being careful not to draw unnecessary attention to the child or making the child feel uncomfortable.

All staff need to use similar methods of recording and to share the responsibility for this. In some establishments diagrams of children's bodies may be available to help you record the location and pattern of injuries accurately.

You may ask the child about the injury, if she can communicate with language. Keep it brief and open-ended, saying, for example, 'What a nasty burn on your arm! Can you remember how you got it?' Record the child's answer and general response. Do not probe any further or push for an explanation, as this may distress the child.

Where there are no physical signs of abuse, the issue is less clear cut, but nonetheless you might feel uneasy about the way a child has started to behave. It would be sensible to keep a diary over a period of time, noting any incidents, accidents or problems that the child has experienced, recording any anxieties or fears that he has confided in you, and noting carefully any absences, especially if these are for a week or more. These records should be dated and completely factual, containing no hearsay or opinions, and completed within 24 hours. You should inform your line manager that you are keeping these records. Remember that parents are entitled to see these records and observations if they so wish. If there has been abuse, you will be asked to produce your written notes at a child protection conference or even in court.

Anywhere Nursery

Name   Date of birth   Start date   Class/group

Date Time	Incident	Physical injury	Non attendance	Conversation	Behaviour causing concern	Action	Signature

Example of a record sheet

Anywhere Nursery

Name Jane Smith   Date of birth 10.3.00   Start date 8.9.03   Class/group Nursery

Date Time	Incident	Physical injury	Non attendance	Conversation	Behaviour causing concern	Action	Signature
30.9.03 10 am		Bruises seen on both arms		Child states she fell off bike		Chart started	CAH
9.10.03 9.30 am 12.15 pm	Child very hungry Asked for food at 9.30 am. Had 3 helpings at lunch					noted	CAH
15.10.03 –26.10.03			F.T.A	Mother states child unwell Did not see G.P.		Discussed with Line Manager	CAH JF
29.10.03 all day				Avoids contact with adults & peers	Quiet, withdrawn Passive	Observations to be made over next week	CAH
16.11.03 3.30 pm	Mother collects child, smells of drink					Discussed with Line Manager	CAH
17.11.03 11 am		? small burns on legs		No response from child	Crying in home corner	Discussed with Line Manager Designated teacher involved	CAH
17.11.03			F.T.A			To contact Social Services	JF

Example of a completed record sheet

7 How to use your observations

This chapter covers:

- In the centre
- In the placement
- Objectivity
- Sharing information
- Compiling a portfolio
- Progression of skills
- Self-appraisal
- Presentation
- Bibliography
- Using your observations in your future professional role

Learning outcomes

Your observation portfolio is an important part of your final assessment but, even more than this, it will show how skilled you have become as a practitioner in integrating your knowledge and understanding of children with your practical skills. A well-presented portfolio will demonstrate your professional approach to your work. Even after you qualify, you should retain your portfolio, as it will demonstrate to prospective employers your competence with young children.

In the centre

As soon as you have finished your first observation and it has been signed in the placement as a true record, you will hand it to your tutor to read, sign and comment on. This should be a regular process, so that you are observing children routinely. It is easier for supervisors and tutors to comment and help you if the observations are presented systematically, in small numbers, after each placement week. Observations given to your supervisor months after the event may well be forgotten and your supervisor might refuse to sign them. Tutors like to see work every time you come back to your centre so that they can pick up on any problems you might be having with the children or in the placement generally.

Many centres use observations to form the basis of group discussion. You will read out your observation, and the group will have a chance to comment on it and help you, perhaps with your interpretation. Your tutor will make sure that you are all on the right path in your interpretations and a great deal will be learned about good practice, individual behaviour and developmental norms. This is an excellent way of integrating theory with practice.

As you progress, your tutor will use some of this time to explain different techniques and methods of recording information. At times, the group will be encouraged to use a particular technique, so that you will obtain immediate feedback in the centre. Your longitudinal studies will need to be carefully monitored, probably on a one-to-one basis with your tutor.

If you should have personal problems that prevent you completing the number of observations required, you should discuss this as soon as you can with your tutor. Never be tempted to invent observations or forge signatures. This would undoubtedly lead to your failing the course.

In the placement

Sometimes, in discussion with your supervisor, you will find that you have observed some behaviour or identified a need of which the placement has not been

Demonstrating gross motor skills

aware. Your observations might then become part of planning an individual programme for the child to help overcome the problem. Occasionally, students' observations have been used at case conferences and have helped to identify issues concerning child protection. In other cases, observations have pointed out that a young child is reading fluently, and encouragement can then be given to the child to extend this skill.

Since the Education Reform Act of 1988, which set out the National Curriculum, all educational establishments are required to keep records and assessments of children at a number of key stages, and you may be asked for a copy of some observations to be placed in the child's file. The Education Act of 1981 initiated statements of special educational need, and your observations may be used for helping with assessment.

Sometimes a placement might not always display good practice in one particular area, and this might be demonstrated in your observation. You will then have to make a difficult decision as to whether to show this observation to your supervisor or not. If you have any suspicion that any child might be at risk, the best policy would be to discuss the observation with your supervisor/tutor and ask for guidance and advice.

Activity

In small groups, carry out a role play showing how you would discuss with the supervisor an observation that a childcare practitioner was not using appropriate language with a child.

List the advantages and disadvantages of raising this with the supervisor.

Objectivity

You have learned not to be subjective when writing and interpreting your observations. Always avoid stereotyping children when setting up structured observations and when taking part in general discussion in the placement. For example, if asked by your centre to observe doll play, you would make sure that you did not invite only the girls to take part. Beware of preconceptions, for example of a child who comes from a family with multiple problems and is observed exhibiting aggressive behaviour. A parent may remark, 'What can you expect? His brothers and sisters were just the same.' Do not fall into the trap of scapegoating this child or indulging in gossip.

Sharing information

All of your observations will be seen by your supervisor and tutor, and you might want to share some observations with parents. You will need to work with parents when carrying out longitudinal studies, as there are obviously periods of time when the child is not in the placement and you might want to know, for example, how the child spends the rest of the time at home, what her appetite is like, and how well she sleeps. If the child is going through a period when her behaviour is erratic it is essential to discuss this with your supervisor, who may give you permission to share this with the parent so that you can all act together to help the child.

You must always be aware of the issue of confidentiality, and some observations should not be generally available to all staff in the placement. If in doubt, your supervisor will provide guidance. Observations should not be left lying around, but stored in a secure place.

Occasionally, observations will be seen by other professional workers outside the placement. For example, language samples might be very useful to speech therapists. You should make these available only with the knowledge and permission of the supervisor. Professional people all act within their code of professional conduct and obviously understand the need for confidentiality.

Compiling a portfolio

For many students, your observation folder will be assessed by the external verifier towards the end of your training. The material must be easy for the verifier to read and follow and therefore you need to organise your work systematically. Regular completion of the observation checklist on page 170 will allow you to monitor your progress.

Routinely, look at your portfolio and count the total of completed observations across the age and technique range. 'Completed' observations are those signed by your supervisor and tutor. At the same time, count the number signed by your supervisor, but not yet handed back to you by your tutor, and the number of observations that you have in rough form still to be written up. The observation checklist allows you to see at a glance where you might have to do further observations.

Verifiers are looking for evidence that you have a true understanding of children's normal development, and that your interpretations demonstrate sensitivity to children's needs. Any observations that show stereotypical attitudes or inappropriate assessments are most likely to be found at the beginning of the course and should be removed from the file.

There is a specified number of observations and assessments that have to be completed. There is also a need to cover a range of methods and types of observation. Your tutor or assessor will indicate to you the requirements of your particular course or qualification.

Observation checklist

Date:

Age group	Total signed by supervisor/tutor	Total signed by supervisor and handed in	No. to be written up	Total
0 to 1 year				
1 to 3:11 years				
4 to 7:11 years				
Other				
Types of observations				
Written record: structured				
Written record: free				
Time sample				
Event sample				
Checklists				
Graphs				
Pie and bar charts				
Histograms				
Target Child				
Longitudinal studies				
Sociograms				
Movement and flow charts				
Language tape				
Group observation				
Individual observation				
Other				

You may photocopy this sheet for your own use. © Nelson Thornes Ltd.

A Practical Guide to Child Observation and Assessment

Range of observations

Once you start building up a portfolio of observations, you must be careful to include a full range. All observations need to be child centred, and focused on the child or children. Adults will often figure in your observations, but it is the reaction of the child to the adult that you need to note.

You will need to:

- Demonstrate that you have covered every area of child development, care and education.
- Cover a range of learning situations, activities, routines and experiences, reflecting the importance of play and language in children's lives and development. Make sure you demonstrate a variety of play situations, such as solo play, messy play, parallel play, group play, creative play, imaginative play, and so on. Language and interaction should be observed between child and adult, and child to child, showing reported speech, understanding and social interaction, such as you might observe during the routine of story time.
- Cover a range of types and patterns of behaviour, to include an emotional range from withdrawn behaviour to aggressive disruptive behaviour. Make sure you include the full spectrum, and do not just concentrate on extremes.
- Observe all the age ranges.
- Ensure that you complete observations in all your placements.

One-to-one communication

- Show aspects of physical care and routines such as washing, feeding, dealing with accidents, caring for the sick child, toilet training, etc., and healthcare routines such us screening and surveillance, immunisation, and so on.
- Cover situations indoors and outdoors in the placement.
- Cover large and small groups and the individual child.
- Cover children's learning and development within the context of the National Curriculum, showing the growth of early literacy, numeracy and scientific understanding.
- Include some children with particular needs, such as distressed children, gifted children and children with special educational needs.
- Cover major events and transitions in children's lives, such as settling into nursery school, birth of a sibling, loss of a parent, etc.
- If possible, observe children whose first language is not English, and attempt to include children from a wide range of different backgrounds within all your placements.
- Use as many different relevant methods of observations as you can.

There may be other areas of special interest to you, or relating to your placement, that you wish to observe and record. If you have any doubts about the suitability of such observations, it would be sensible to discuss this with your tutor.

Progression of skills

Completion of a portfolio of observations will allow you to become a professional expert at observation techniques, and you will be much valued for this skill in many multi-disciplinary teams. It is by no means an easy skill to develop and you may take quite a while before you feel really comfortable in demonstrating your techniques. Your centre will devote time each week to help you gain confidence and your placement will allow you adequate time to practise your skills. In building up your portfolio you will progress from simple structured written records of one child over a short period of time to complex techniques observing groups of children over several weeks. Your increasing skills will be demonstrated in your work and will be acknowledged by the external moderation process .

Self-appraisal

From time to time you might find it useful to look at your observations and assess them for yourself. Having carried out this task, it is occasionally a good idea to check your self-appraisal with that of your tutor and your supervisor.

One way of grading this could be to give yourself a mark of 5 for excellence, 4 for very good, 3 for satisfactory, 2 for could do better and 1 for unsatisfactory.

Having completed the appraisal, you may be able to identify the areas where you need to seek help in order to progress. In discussion with your tutor or assessor

Self-appraisal checklist

Date:

	You	Your tutor	Your supervisor
Number of observations			
Range across the areas of development			
Range across the age groups			
Range of techniques			
Choosing appropriate observations			
Presented in a professional manner			
Awareness of strict confidentiality			
Making progress in interpreting observations			
Working systematically – setting aside time each week			
Seeking help in difficulty			
Accepting and acting on constructive criticism			

Questions to ask yourself:

Are you up to date?

Are you finding the process is becoming easier?

What areas do you find easy?

What areas do you find difficult?

you may develop an action plan together. For example, if you have difficulty in using one particular method of recording, your supervisor or assessor might be able to write an observation with you, using this technique. If interpretation is the problem, you might be advised to extend your reading.

Activity

Looking at a recent observation, ask yourself the following questions.

Was the observation technique you used appropriate?

Would another method have given more reliable results?

Did you discover within yourself any preconceived or stereotypical ideas?

Were any strong emotions aroused?

Your course will require you to submit a minimum number of observations at a satisfactory standard. You will need to complete more than the minimum number in order to select those observations that meet the criteria and cover a range of methods and techniques. Aiming for a higher number will allow you to discard some observations that you feel are not up to standard.

Presentation

Observations should be presented in a plain ring folder with your registration and centre numbers only on the outside of the portfolio. Similar paper should be used throughout and it is tidier to use the same colour ink. Many students like to put observations into plastic pockets. Although this keeps them clean and tidy whilst you are storing them, it is not necessary to present them like this in your completed portfolio. In addition to being expensive, it makes the portfolio bulky and sometimes unwieldy to handle. If you have access to a word processor you may prefer to present all or some of your observations typed. Handwritten observations are quite acceptable as long as there are not too many corrected errors and the handwriting is legible. You might find it better to rewrite some of your observations rather than offer untidy, messy work, but bear in mind that you will need to obtain fresh signatures.

It is a good idea to incorporate dividers into the portfolio. They could be used to divide your observations into types of placement, for example 'Nursery school', 'Private family', etc., or into ages: 0 to 1, 1 to 3:11, 4 to 7:11 years. This will help people to use the portfolio and find the age group or placement more easily. All observations should have the standard front page.

All observations must be numbered and in date order within the divisions. This will demonstrate the progress you have made.

A matrix may be provided and should be kept up to date and placed in the front of your file. On some courses you may have to provide a table of contents, such as the following example.

TABLE OF CONTENTS OF OBSERVATION PORTFOLIO

Observation number	Date	Aim	Age(s) gender	Details of setting	Techniques	Individual/ group
1	11.10.03	Emot. dev.	4:2 M	Bathroom	Written record	I
2	13.10.03	Physical skills	3:6 F	Outside area	Written record	I
3	25.10.03	Lang. dev.	4:1F 4:2F 4:6 F	Classroom	Written record	G
4	25.10.03	Fine phys. dev.	3:6 M	Classroom	Written record	I
5	7.11.03 & 8.11.03	Emot. dev.	4:6 F	Nursery class	Time sample	I
6	22.11.03	Physical skills	3:2 M	Nursery class	Checklist	I

Bibliography

This refers to the reading you have done in order to interpret your observations. At the end of most of your observations you will have put a list, naming the books and authors which helped you with your analysis. You need to list the books/articles in alphabetical order of author, followed by the date and title of the book or article and the publisher. For example:

Dare A. and O'Donovan M., 2003, *A Practical Guide to Child Nutrition*, 2nd edition, Nelson Thornes.
Lindon J., 23 October 1997, 'Babies on Board' in *Nursery World*.

When you have completed your file, you will be asked to sign a statement declaring the authenticity of the work.

Table of Contents of Observation Portfolio

Observation number	Date	Aim	Age(s) gender	Details of setting	Techniques	Individual/ group

You may photocopy this sheet for your own use. © Nelson Thornes Ltd.

A Practical Guide to Child Observation and Assessment

Using your observations in your future professional role

As a student, you might have initially thought that doing observations was an obstacle that you were expected to surmount in order to gain your qualification. We are confident that by the time you have completed the course you will have become proficient in this skill and be fully informed of how important observing children closely is to your awareness and understanding of their needs and development.

You will find that you will use observations and assessments in many different situations. These will vary from routine to structured assessments in cases of particular need. Observations will help in planning the curriculum and ensuring the most effective use of the learning environment.

Whatever area of childcare employment or future training you enter, observing children will be an integral part of your professional role. By using observations, you will get to know the children in your care in an objective manner and be able to plan suitable routines and individual activities, so as to extend their development and understand their total needs. Childcare practitioners are regarded by many other professionals as the experts in using observational techniques and contributing to their interpretation so as to help all children to fulfil their potential.

Good practice for the childcare practitioner

1 Respect confidentiality.
2 Keep files in a secure place.
3 Be ready to share observations and assessments with parents as this strengthens partnerships with parents.
4 Be systematic in your recording, making sure that all children are observed regularly.
5 Always be objective.
6 Never jump to conclusions, labelling children, generalising behaviour from one sample or guessing why children respond in a particular manner.
7 Allow for environmental and cultural differences, whilst all the time guarding against racist and sexist attitudes.
8 When directly assessing a child, be careful not to involve yourself in the activity, or to influence the child's behaviour by your manner or tone of voice.
9 Write up your observation notes promptly, so as to give as clear a record as possible of what took place.
10 Use your observations for the benefit of the children and to develop good practice within the workplace.
11 Use your observations with children to help them reflect on their own development and learning.
12 Keep up to date with current research, reading and techniques and be prepared to consider new methods of assessment as they become available.
13 Observations should link assessment of the child's progress with planning the curriculum and routines in the establishment.
14 All observations should reflect anti-bias practice.

Appendix 1: Developmental norms

Developmental norms 0 to 1 year

	Physical development – gross motor	Physical development – fine motor	Social and emotional development	Cognitive and language development
At birth	Reflexes: • Rooting, sucking and swallowing reflex • Grasp reflex • Walking reflex • Moro reflex If pulled to sit, head falls backwards If held in sitting position, head falls forward, and back is curved In supine (laying on back), limbs are bent In prone (laying on front), lies in fetal position with knees tucked up Unable to raise head or stretch limbs	Reflexes • Pupils reacting to light • Opens eyes when held upright • Blinks or opens eyes wide to sudden sound • Startle reaction to sudden sound • Closing eyes to sudden bright light	Bonding/attachment	Cries vigorously, with some variation in pitch and duration
1 month	In prone, lifts chin In supine, head moves to one side Arm and leg extended on face side Begins to flex upper and lower limbs	Hands fisted Eyes move to dangling objects	Watches mother's face with increasingly alert facial expression Fleeting smile – may be wind! Stops crying when picked up	Cries become more differentiated to indicate needs Stops and attends to voice, rattle and bell
3 months	Held sitting, head straight back and neck firm. Lower back still weak When lying, pelvis is flat	Grasps an object when placed in hand Turns head right round to look at objects Eye contact firmly established	Reacts with pleasure to familiar situations/routines	Regards hands with intense interest Beginning to vocalise

continued

Developmental norms 0 to 1 year continued

	Physical development – gross motor	Physical development – fine motor	Social and emotional development	Cognitive and language development
6 months	In supine, can lift head and shoulders In prone, can raise up on hands Sits with support Kicks strongly May roll over When held, enjoys standing and jumping	Has learned to grasp objects and passes toys from hand to hand Visual sense well established	Takes everything to mouth Responds to different emotional tones of chief caregiver	Finds feet interesting Vocalises tunefully Laughs in play Screams with annoyance Understands purpose of rattle
9 months	Sits unsupported Begins to crawl Pulls to stand, falls back with bump	Visually attentive Grasps with thumb and index finger Releases toy by dropping Looks for fallen objects Beginning to finger-feed Holds bottle or cup	Plays peek-a-boo – can start earlier Imitates hand clapping Clings to familiar adults, reluctant to go to strangers – from about 7 months	Watches activities of others with interest Vocalises to attract attention Beginning to babble Finds partially hidden toy Shows an interest in picture books Knows own name
1 year	Walks holding one hand, may walk alone Bends down and picks up objects Pulls to stand and sits deliberately	Picks up small objects Fine pincer grip Points at objects Holds spoon	Co-operates in dressing Demonstrates affection Participates in nursery rhymes Waves bye bye	Uses jargon Responds to simple instructions and understands several words Puts wooden cubes in and out of cup or box

Developmental norms 1 to 3:11 years

	Physical development – gross motor	Physical development – fine motor	Social and emotional development	Cognitive and language development
1 year	Walks holding one hand, may walk alone Bends down and picks up objects Pulls to stand and sits deliberately	Picks up small objects Fine pincer grip Points at objects Holds spoon	Co-operates in dressing Demonstrates affection Participates in nursery rhymes Waves bye bye	Uses jargon Responds to simple instructions and understands several words Puts wooden cubes in and out of cup or box
15 months	Walking usually well established Can crawl up stairs frontwards and down stairs backwards Kneels unaided Balance poor; falls heavily	Holds crayon with palmar grasp Precise pincer grasp, both hands Builds tower of 2 cubes Can place objects precisely Uses spoon which sometimes rotates Turns pages of picture book	Indicates wet or soiled pants Helps with dressing Emotionally dependent on familiar adult	Jabbers loudly and freely, with 2–6 recognisable words, and can communicate needs Intensely curious Reproduces lines drawn by adult
18 months	Climbs up and down stairs with hand held Runs carefully Pushes, pulls and carries large toys Backs into small chair Can squat to pick up toys	Builds tower of 3 cubes Scribbles to and fro spontaneously Begins to show preference for one hand Drinks without spilling	Tries to sing Imitates domestic activities Bowel control sometimes attained Alternates between clinging and resistance Plays contentedly alone near familiar adult	Enjoys simple picture books, recognising some characters Jabbering established 6–20 recognisable words May use echolalia (repeating adult's last word, or last word of rhyme) Is able to show several parts of the body, when asked Explores environment energetically
2 years	Runs with confidence, avoiding obstacles Walks up and down stairs both feet to each step, holding wall Squats with ease. Rises without using hands Can climb up on furniture and get down again Steers tricycle pushing along with feet Throws small ball overarm, and kicks large ball	Turns picture book pages one at at time Builds tower of 6 cubes Holds pencil with first 2 fingers and thumb near to point	Competently spoon feeds and drinks from cup Is aware of physical needs Can put on shoes and hat Keenly interested in outside environment – unaware of dangers Demands chief caregiver's attention and often clings Parallel play Throws tantrums if frustrated	Identifies photographs of familiar adults Identifies small world toys Recognises tiny details in pictures Uses own name to refer to self Speaks in 2- and 3-word sentences, and can sustain short conversations Asks for names and labels Talks to self continuously

continued

Developmental norms 1 to 3:11 years continued

	Physical development – gross motor	Physical development – fine motor	Social and emotional development	Cognitive and language development
3 years	Competent locomotive skills	Cuts paper with scissors	Uses spoon and fork	Can copy a circle and some letters
	Can jump off lower steps	Builds a tower of 9 cubes and a bridge with 3 cubes	Increased independence in self care	Can draw a person with a head and 2 other parts of the body
	Still uses 2 feet to a step coming down stairs	Good pencil control	Dry day and night	May name colours and match 3 primary colours
	Pedals and steers tricycle	Can thread 3 large beads on a string	Affectionate and co-operative	Speech and comprehension well established
			Plays co-operatively, particularly domestic play	Some immature pronunciations and unconventional grammatical forms
			Tries to please	Asks questions constantly
				Can give full name, gender and age
				Relates present activities and past experiences
				Increasing interest in words and numbers
4 years	All motor muscles well controlled	Builds a tower of 10 cubes	Boasts and is bossy	Draws person with head, legs and trunk
	Can turn sharp corners when running	Uses 6 cubes to build 3 steps, when shown	Sense of humour developing	Draws recognisable house
	Hops on favoured foot		Cheeky, answers back	Uses correct grammar most of the time
	Balances for 3–5 seconds		Wants to be independent	Most pronunciations mature
	Increasing skill at ball games		Plans games co-operatively	Ask meanings of words
	Sits with knees crossed		Argues with other children but learning to share	Enjoys verses and jokes, and may use swear words
				Counts up to 20
				Imaginative play well developed

Developmental norms 4 to 7:11 years

	Physical development – gross motor	Physical development – fine motor	Social and emotional development	Cognitive and language development
4 years	All motor muscles well controlled	Builds a tower of 10 cubes	Boasts and is bossy	Draws person with head, legs and trunk
	Can turn sharp corners when running	Uses 6 cubes to build 3 steps. when shown	Sense of humour developing	Draws recognisable house
	Hops on favoured foot		Cheeky, answers back	Uses correct grammar most of the time
	Balances for 3–5 seconds		Wants to be independent	Most pronunciations mature
	Increasing skill at ball games		Plans games co-operatively	Asks meanings of words
	Sits with knees crossed		Argues with other children but learning to share	Enjoys verses and jokes, and may use swear words
				Counts up to 20
				Imaginative play well developed
5 years	Can touch toes keeping legs straight	Threads needle and sews	Copes well with daily personal needs	Matches most colours
	Hops on either foot	Builds steps with 3–4 cubes	Chooses own friends	Copies square, triangle and several letters, writing some unprompted
	Skips	Colours pictures carefully	Well-balanced and sociable	Writes name
	Runs on toes	Can copy adult writing	Sense of fair play and understanding of rules developing	Draws a detailed person
	Ball skills developing well		Shows caring attitudes towards others	Speaks correctly and fluently
	Can walk along a thin line			Knows home address
				Able and willing to complete projects
				Understands numbers using concrete objects
				Imaginary play now involves make-believe games

continued

A Practical Guide to Child Observation and Assessment

Developmental norms 4 to 7:11 years continued

	Physical development – gross motor	Physical development – fine motor	Social and emotional development	Cognitive and language development
6 years	Jumps over rope 25 cm high Learning to skip with rope	Ties own shoe laces	Eager for fresh experiences More demanding and stubborn, less sociable Joining a 'gang' may be important May be quarrelsome with friends Needs to succeed as failing too often leads to poor self-esteem	Reading skills developing well Drawings more precise and detailed Figure may be drawn in profile Can describe how one object differs from another Mathematical skills developing, may use symbols instead of concrete objects May write independently
7 years	Rides a 2-wheel bicycle Improved balance	Skills constantly improving More dexterity and precision in all areas	Special friend at school Peer approval becoming important Likes to spend some time alone Enjoys TV and books May be moody May attempt tasks too complex to complete	Moving towards abstract thought Able to read Can give opposite meanings Able to write a paragraph independently
8–12 years	Movements well co-ordinated Physical skills improving Takes part in team games with equipment Swims	Skills constantly improving Drawings become more complex	Friendships become more important Independence increasing More understanding of self	Concentration improves Able to read fluently Can write a story May think scientifically Able to play complex games such as chess
12–16 years	Hormonal changes Puberty Skin changes Growth spurts Body hair develops Girl: menstruates; breasts develop: hips broaden Boys: facial hair develops; voice deepens; growth of penis and testes	Skills develop depending on interest and practice, for example playing guitar, Nintendo games, model making	Mood swings May rebel against authority Interest in sex begins May experiment with different identities	Adolescents start to think about the future and if motivated will use all their intellectual ability to achieve their educational goals

Appendix 2: Resources

Books and articles

Bartholomew L. and Bruce T., 1993, *Getting to Know You: A Guide to Record Keeping in Early Education and Care*, Hodder and Stoughton.

Beaty Janice J., 1998, *Observing Development of the Young Child*, 4th edition, Prentice Hall.

Bee H., 1995, *The Growing Child*, HarperCollins.

Bee H., 1997, *The Developing Child*, 8th edition, Addison-Wesley.

Blenkin G. and Kelly A. (eds), 1992, *Assessment in Early Childhood Education*, Paul Chapman.

Brown B., 1998, *Unlearning Discrimination in the Early Years*, Trentham Books.

Clarke S., 1998, *Targeting Assessment: The Primary Classroom*, Hodder Arnold.

Clemson D. and Clemson W., 1996, *The Really Practical Guide to Primary Assessment*, 2nd edition, Stanley Thornes.

Drummond M., 2003, *Assessing Children's Learning*, David Fulton Press.

Drummond M. and Nutbrown C., 1992, 'Observing and Assessing Young Children' in *Contemporary Issues in the Early Years*, ed. G. Pugh, NCB/Paul Chapman.

Drummond M., Rouse D. and Pugh G., 1992, *Making Assessment Work*, NES Arnold/NCB.

Fawcett M., 1996, *Learning through Child Observation*, Jessica Kingsley.

Goldschmied E. and Selleck D., 1996, *Communication between Babies in Their First Year*, National Children's Bureau. (A video is included with this training book.)

Hall D. et al., 1994, *The Child Surveillance Handbook*, 2nd edition, Radcliffe Medical Press.

Hobart C. and Frankel J., 1998, *Good Practice in Child Protection*, Stanley Thornes.

Hobart C. and Frankel J., 1999, *A Practical Guide to Activities for Young Children*, 2nd edition, Stanley Thornes.

Malik H., 1998, *A Practical Guide to Equal Opportunities*, Stanley Thornes.

Millam R., 1996, *Anti-discriminatory Practice*, Cassell.

Miller L. et al., 1989, *Closely Observed Infants*, Duckworth.

O'Hagan M. and Smith M., 1999, *Special Issues in Childcare*, Baillière Tindall.

Quilham S., 1994, *Child Watching: A Parent's Guide to Body Language*, Ward Lock.

Sheridan M., 1997, *From Birth to Five Years* (revised and updated by M. Frost and A. Sharma), Routledge.

Sheridan M. 1999, *Play in Early Childhood: From Birth to Six Years*, Routledge.

Sylva K. et al., 1980, *Childwatching at Playgroup and Nursery School*, Grant McIntyre.

Wolfenden S., 1990, *All About Me*, NES Arnold.

Videos

Child Observations, Siren Films, Video Ltd, 5 Charlotte Square, Newcastle-upon-Tyne, NE1 4XF. Telephone 01912 327900. Baby study outline.

Organisations

Data Protection, Information Commissioner's Office, Wycliffe House, Water Lane, Wilmslow, Cheshire SK9 5AF.

Packs

SureStart: Birth to Three Matters. Pack avaliable from DfeS publication department, PO Box 5050, Sherwood Park, Annesley, Nottingham NG15 0DJ. Telephone 0845 6022260.

Index

Page references in *italics* indicate illustrations and diagrams, those in **bold** indicate tables, charts or forms.